Music
Success
In Nine Weeks

A Step-By-Step Guide
On How to Use Social Media & Online Tactics
to Supercharge your PR Build Your Fan Base
And Earn More Money

By Ariel Hyatt

Music Success In Nine Weeks: A Step-By-Step Guide On How to Use Social Media & Online Tactics to Supercharge your PR Build Your Fan Base And Earn More Money .

Copyright (c) 2009 by Ariel Hyatt

Published by Ariel Publicity, Artist Relations and Booking LLC, 389 12th Street, Brooklyn NY 11215.

Visit our website at: www.arielpublicity.com.

Email us at: contact@arielpublicity.com.

Designed by Adam Williams
www.sleepy.me.uk

MUSIC SUCCESS IN NINE WEEKS

A STEP-BY-STEP GUIDE ON HOW TO USE SOCIAL MEDIA & ONLINE TACTICS TO SUPERCHARGE YOUR PR BUILD YOUR FAN BASE AND EARN MORE MONEY

BY ARIEL HYATT

INTRODUCTION

You are taking a big step in your music career by purchasing this book.

I am excited to share this information with you. It is the culmination of my 16 years experience working in the music industry as a music publicist, observing and handling over 1,400 PR and marketing campaigns, primarily for independent musicians.

Over the years I've noticed something that seems to separate the artists that I have represented into two categories.

The artists in the first category (Group A) have experienced dramatic increases in their fan bases, and have seen palpable results as their careers grew. They consistently created more income and got more exposure. I'm going to call these bands the **Builders** because their careers are expanding.

The artists in the second category (Group B) gained more PR exposure (because they hired me to get them PR) so that worked, but they did not see a dramatic increase in their fan bases nor did their income increase. I call this group the **Idlers**.

The interesting thing is that the artists in Group A were no better musically than the artists in Group B.

I can say, however, that the artists in Group A were more tenacious: they never took no for an answer, they never gave up and they worked harder and complained less than the artists in Group B. **Builders** knew something that the **Idlers** did not know. I have outlined what they knew and the actions they took, and I will explain how they achieved success and more traction step-by-step in this book.

This program is designed to make you a **Builder** and not an **Idler**.

By agreeing to become a student of the rapidly changing Internet - which has become, in my humble opinion, the indisputable future of the music business - and by following this 9-week program, I promise that you will see results.

This system works!

How do I know?

I have tested it all with my own business – and it has made and continues to make a huge difference.

Running an indie music PR firm is a lot like directing an indie music career.

Like you, I have events, a newsletter and fans, and I also need to consistently develop a following in order to keep my dream alive.

Much like my artists, I work tirelessly to keep my dream afloat. What you are about to read and implement over the next nine weeks has successfully increased my income over the past few years. It will also increase yours.

This 9-week course is a process that will take some time and effort to implement. And, you may not actually be able to get it done in nine weeks flat. Some of these steps may take you longer, and that's okay. I implore you to not get overwhelmed and feel as though you must do everything outlined here all at once. If you put one foot in front of the other, you will get results.

There is a lot to learn in this program; as my friend and co-conspirator Derek Sivers, founder of *CD Baby*, brilliantly advises: Don't force yourself to do the things that you hate.

I have ideas throughout this book to help you outsource and offload the things you really detest and don't want to do… but here's another observation I have made over the years: Artists who have experience *trying* to do things they don't enjoy, tackling and completing them at least once, are able to oversee these tasks much more effectively when the time comes to let other people handle them.

However, that being said, if something in these modules gives you that horrible feeling in the pit of your stomach, then outsource it to another member of the band, your biggest fan or your mom, but don't be Sisyphus and try to push a boulder up the mountain – we all know what happened to him. Take this program one step at a time. The best results will happen if you read each module and implement it in the order outlined in the book.

Here's to your success!

Ariel

MASTERMIND FORUM

This book comes with lifetime membership and access to my closed online Mastermind Forum for **Extra Support.**

On it you will be able to walk yourself through the steps in a group forum, get access to me and to my staff at Cyber PR and get valuable feedback.

To sign up send an email to Contact@ArielPublicity.com to get a link for your membership, with the subject line **"I bought the book!"** and you will receive a link for your account.

DEDICATION

To every single musician I have ever worked with.

You have given me your trust and your hard-earned money, and you have allowed me to help you with your art. Most of all, you have filled my life with the most joyful expression of humanity: Music.

Thank you for allowing me to live my dream.

It has been an honor and a pleasure to be of service.

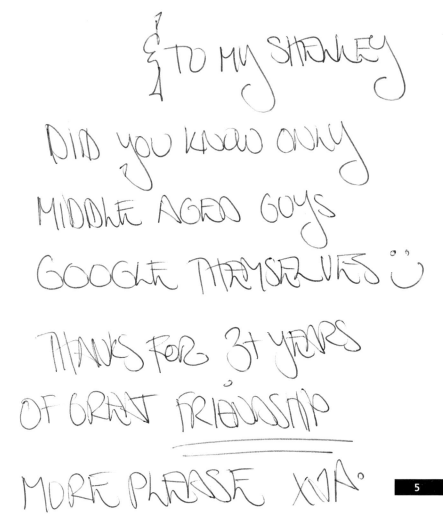

TO MY SHIRLEY

DID YOU KNOW ONLY MIDDLE AGED GUYS GOOGLE THEMSELVES :)

THANKS FOR 3+ YEARS OF GREAT FRIENDSHIP

MORE PLEASE XXX

ACKNOWLEDGEMENTS

To: My Mother – Who blazed the trail, which is bright, wide-open, and ready for me to walk.

To: My Father – Who makes me laugh every step of the way.

To: Enid – For teaching me patience and for all of your love.

To: Kristin Fayne-Mulroy – For your editing skills and your input, and for being my best friend since kindergarten.

To: Derek Sivers – For constantly sharing your great ideas, and for being my sounding board in this amazing music business.

CONTENTS

WEEK 1: GETTING MENTALLY PREPARED

Before we dive into the full nine week program of getting into action and learning new things, I want to help put you in the right frame of mind to tackle it all.

This portion of the book is supposed to be fun and creative. Do not look at this like an assignment – think of it as creatively as you can, like writing a song.

Make sure you have a notebook available where you can keep all of your notes. I suggest writing these exercises out by hand; however, if you take notes on a computer, create a separate folder so you can refer to them later.

SETTING GOALS

Starting this program with a clear set of goals is an empowering way to set the stage for your success.

This section will assist you in creating a personal roadmap for achieving your goals in your musical career, whether music is your hobby or your full-time living.

ITEMS YOU WILL NEED:

1. A blank notebook / your diary / journal. (If you don't have one on hand right this moment it's OK – buy one ASAP.)

2. Several pieces (10 – 12) of blank paper.

3. Colored pens, crayons, or watercolors.

4. An inspiring place – your studio, home, a coffee shop etc.

An Astounding Fact – ONLY 3%

Only three percent of all people have their long-term goals written down, and it has been proven that by simply writing down your goals you are much more likely to achieve them.

I Repeat—Just By Completing This Exercise You Are MUCH More Likely to Achieve Your Goals.

Dr. Edward Banfield of Harvard University concluded, after more than 50 years of research, that long-term perspective is the most accurate single predictor of upward social and economic mobility in America. It is more important than family background, education, race, intelligence, and connections in determining your success in life and work.

And IT WORKS!

Goal setting is the most powerful thing I did for myself last year. In January, I wrote down what I wanted to achieve for the year, both personally and for my business. Every month I wrote down what I had achieved, or checked something off the list when I completed it. Just by writing out, measuring my goals, and continuously keeping them in front of me, I made them happen!

GOAL ACHIEVING TIP # 1:
THIS IS A GAME; YOU CAN CHANGE THE RULES AS YOU GO

Goals are not written in stone and they are not the word of the Almighty. They should be looked at as beacons and guiding points to help keep you on track along your journey.

While I would not recommend changing your goals every week, the music industry is changing so rapidly it's hard to know what goals are reachable in this landscape. So if in the course of the year your goals change, it's okay to cross one off, modify another, or start the game again and write new ones down as you go.

GOAL ACHIEVING TIP #2: DON'T BEAT YOURSELF UP!

Implementing these goals freely will take a whole year, so be patient. You will have days where you may get frustrated, and you will start to beat yourself up. This is something I see *a lot* of my musicians do.

One client I represent will play an amazing set, get offstage, and all of a sudden start ripping into himself saying it sucked, or the sound was awful, or he couldn't hear himself, or he screwed up the entire second verse.

Sound familiar?

This kind of self-criticism will interfere directly with achieving your goals and dreams.

So, the next time you are making yourself wrong for the bad note you hit or the drummer who was late to rehearsal... take a step back and try to take a moment to acknowledge the good, and even – gasp! – celebrate the wins.

GOAL ACHIEVING TIP #3: FIVE SUCCESSES EACH DAY

I'm inviting you to write down five little victories a day not only for the coming nine weeks but for an entire year, starting right now.

WRITTEN EXERCISE: YOUR FIVE SUCCESSES

I learned this powerful technique from T. Harv Eker, author of the *Secrets of the Millionaire Mind.*

He says that you should write down five positive things you do every single day. Once you start getting into this habit, you are training yourself to put the focus on the positive and get your mind to stop being so self-critical.

So put a notebook in your gig bag or next to your bed and throughout this nine weeks, write down five successes each day.

Make at least one or two of them music career related.

Here are some examples:

1. Went to gym

2. Started writing lyrics to that song I've been thinking about

3. Called three clubs for potential bookings

4. Did laundry

5. Reached out to a music blogger who will love my music

6. Made dinner for my boyfriend/girlfriend/husband/wife/kids

7. Added my band's profile on a website

If you keep a journal or a notebook where you write lyrics, use that; if not, go purchase a blank book to write these in daily. It's amazing to look back over a year and read them all.

YOUR FIRST FIVE SUCCESSES

Right now, stop what you're doing and write down five tiny successes you had from today and yesterday.

1

2

3

4

5

DAY 2 SUCCESSES

1

2

3

4

5

WRITTEN EXERCISE: GOAL SETTING

I suggest you write in pen using paper.

Your intention manifests differently when it comes from a pen and not from a computer. The act of writing it down accesses a different part of your brain and it makes a deal between your hand, your mind and your heart.

WRITE DOWN YOUR FOCUS AREAS

Here is a list of some areas you may want to focus on. Skip the ones that are not for you and write out a goal in each area. Think big, be unreasonable, and don't hold yourself back.

Write Down At Least Six Focus Areas – Here Are A Few Ideas To Jump Start Your Brain:

- Branding – Creating a solid pitch and USP (unique selling point)

- Marketing – What will you do this year for your marketing plan?

- Online and Social Media strategies?

- Does your Website need a re-design in the next few months?

- PR – Getting covered on radio, online, TV, print media – write down where you see yourself reaching out for PR?

- Booking – Touring or local gigs?

- Music Conferences – Will you attend or play any?

- Writing songs? How many? Recording an album this year? In a studio or at home? How many tracks?

- Number of CDs/downloads you would like to sell?

- How much money you would like to earn?

- Film and TV placements – Will you focus on these?

- Building your fan base – How will you do this?

- How many people should be added to your e-mail list?

- Number of people at your next gig (write an exact number).

- Number of people at each gig for the next 12 months.

- Getting a manager / booking agent.

- Buying a new instrument.

- Having friends or family members get involved with helping you

- Personal health so your performance is better – exercise, nutrition, etc.

- Mental health – positive frame of mind, meditation, time away, etc.

BEFORE YOU GET STARTED:

Techniques For Writing Down Goals

1. Be really clear about your goals – give dates by when you will achieve them, and describe them in as much detail as you can. Visualize and write each one as if it's already happening.

2. Your goals should involve you and only you (they can't be contingent on someone else).

3. Make them so they are realistically achievable.

WRITE OUT AT LEAST SIX GOALS HERE:

1

2

3

4

5

GETTING GOALS TO HAPPEN:

Do something every day that moves you towards achieving these goals (your list of five successes each day will help with this).

Make daily lists of tasks you need to complete in order to get your goals met – the night before!

Write out a time frame for each task (15 minutes, 1 hour etc.)

Do the hardest thing first in the morning – don't procrastinate.

Studies show that the average person can achieve six tasks a day so write a MAXIMUM of six per day – don't get overwhelmed.

Delegate the little activities that waste your valuable time to other people (you would be surprised what you could accomplish with the 4 hours it takes to clean your house).

Build a TEAM to help you! Get an intern or two.

Log on to http://www.entertainmentcareers.net and post (for no charge) as an employer seeking interns – There are a lot of bright young people who would like to get their feet wet in the music business. You technically run a record label, so advertise for a label assistant, marketing manager or street team/Social Media director.

If you don't have an office to accommodate them that's okay: meet once a week at a coffee shop or have your intern work remotely from home as a virtual assistant.

GOAL ACHIEVING TIP # 4:
MAKE ONE HAPPEN ASAP

Start with the easiest goal on your list, give it a two to four week deadline, and then write out the goal in the present tense, as if it is already achieved, with a date, like this:

Today is [date], and I have added 25 new quality friends to my Facebook page.

Today is [date] and I have created a Facebook page for my band and invited everyone to join it.

Now, go back and put dates on every single goal you wrote.

Last part of the exercise:

MAKE THE GOALS LOOK PRETTY & HANG THEM WHERE YOU CAN SEE THEM EVERYDAY

I highly recommend re-writing your goals neatly on paper. Use colored pens, watercolors, or crayons and illustrate them. Hang them in a place where you can see them everyday. Remember, if your goals change, that's okay! Just cross one off and add a new one. YOU are the one in charge of YOUR GOALS.

Suggestions:

Keep a few separate lists:

- MUSIC GOALS – Next 12 Months

- MUSIC GOALS – In your lifetime

- MONEY GOALS – Next 12 months

- ANNUAL GOALS – For yourself/family

- LIFETIME GOALS – What do you want in your whole life

Remember to put a date on when you will achieve each goal.

Use the following pages or your own notebook…

MUSIC CAREER GOALS – NEXT 12 MONTHS

DATE WRITTEN:

1.

BY WHEN:

DATE WRITTEN:

2.

BY WHEN:

DATE WRITTEN:

3.

BY WHEN:

DATE WRITTEN:

4.

BY WHEN:

DATE WRITTEN:

5.

BY WHEN:

DATE WRITTEN:

6.

BY WHEN:

MUSIC CAREER GOALS - IN YOUR LIFETIME

DATE WRITTEN:

1.

BY WHEN:

DATE WRITTEN:

2.

BY WHEN:

DATE WRITTEN:

3.

BY WHEN:

DATE WRITTEN:

4.

BY WHEN:

DATE WRITTEN:

5.

BY WHEN:

DATE WRITTEN:

6.

BY WHEN:

$ MONEY GOALS – NEXT 12 MONTHS

DATE WRITTEN:

1.

BY WHEN:

DATE WRITTEN:

2.

BY WHEN:

DATE WRITTEN:

3.

BY WHEN:

DATE WRITTEN:

4.

BY WHEN:

DATE WRITTEN:

5.

BY WHEN:

DATE WRITTEN:

6.

BY WHEN:

ANNUAL GOALS / NEXT 12 MONTHS FOR YOURSELF & YOUR FAMILY

DATE WRITTEN:

1.

BY WHEN:

DATE WRITTEN:

2.

BY WHEN:

DATE WRITTEN:

3.

BY WHEN:

DATE WRITTEN:

4.

BY WHEN:

DATE WRITTEN:

5.

BY WHEN:

DATE WRITTEN:

6.

BY WHEN:

DATE WRITTEN:

7.

BY WHEN:

DATE WRITTEN:

8.

BY WHEN:

DATE WRITTEN:

9.

BY WHEN:

DATE WRITTEN:

10.

BY WHEN:

DATE WRITTEN:

11.

BY WHEN:

DATE WRITTEN:

12.

BY WHEN:

LIFETIME GOALS & INTENTIONS

DATE WRITTEN:

1.

BY WHEN:

DATE WRITTEN:

2.

BY WHEN:

DATE WRITTEN:

3.

BY WHEN:

DATE WRITTEN:

4.

BY WHEN:

DATE WRITTEN:

5.

BY WHEN:

DATE WRITTEN:

6.

BY WHEN:

DATE WRITTEN:

7.

BY WHEN:

DATE WRITTEN:

8.

BY WHEN:

DATE WRITTEN:

9.

BY WHEN:

DATE WRITTEN:

10.

BY WHEN:

DATE WRITTEN:

11.

BY WHEN:

DATE WRITTEN:

12.

BY WHEN:

More... Write them ALL!! THINK BIG!!!!

NOTES

WEEK 2: YOUR PERFECT PITCH

CREATING THE PERFECT PITCH

This week is a key lesson in branding yourself, both online and offline, and will set you up to have a major breakthrough in your musical career. What you create here will define you in the minds of your fans and potential fans.

Two scenarios happened to inspire the writing of this chapter:

SCENARIO #1:

I was out at the Mercury Lounge seeing music, and between bands I was standing at the bar talking to some friends when someone handed me a show flyer. I was taken with him immediately; I always appreciate anyone who is self-promoting because it's not easy to do, and it's especially not easy to do at a crowded bar on a Wednesday night in downtown Manhattan.

So, I looked down at the flyer and my heart sank. It said the following:

Name of artist (not mentioned to protect the innocent)

Venue (which was the Mercury, where I was)

Date and show time

There I was, a perfectly primed potential fan, a customer standing at a bar, out at a live music show, and he lost me forever. Why?

Because not one sentence was included about what genre of music this artist played, much less what his music sounded like or who he was compared to (sound-alike). In short I had no idea what to expect if I came out to his show.

To top it off, there was no website listed on the flyer. On the off-chance that I had taken the flyer home, I would never have known where to listen to his music online.

That was a HUGE opportunity totally LOST. Unbeknownst to him, he also handed his flyer to one of the most successful entertainment attorneys I know (who was in the middle of signing six artists to record deals), an A&R executive, and one of the best booking agents in the business.

We all looked down at the flyers in our hands, shrugged and carried on with our conversation. He had totally BLOWN it.

SCENARIO #2:

The second thing that happened was that an artist called my PR firm to talk about hiring us for a Cyber PR campaign, and two minutes into the conversation I was beginning to feel like he was totally wasting my time. It went something like this:

Me: "What do you sound like?"

Artist: "I sound like absolutely nothing you've ever heard before."

Me: (annoyed and understanding why he's not where he wants to be as an artist) "Really? So you've invented a new genre of music, and you don't sound like anyone else in the history of music?"

Artist: "Yes"

Me: "Can you at least tell me what type of music you play?"

Artist: "It's old school Hip-Hop."

OK, finally we were getting somewhere. Now, while I totally understood his point, here's the problem with having an approach like his:

People are constantly looking for a context to put things into. And if you don't provide them with one, they will move on to the next thing that their little pea brains can actually grasp.

The critical thing that was missing in both scenarios was **The Pitch.**

A pitch is sometimes called your Elevator Pitch (how you can describe yourself in the course of an elevator ride); marketers call it a USP (unique selling point); my friend Bob Baker calls it a BIS (brand identity statement); and Laura Allen, founder of 15secondpitch.com, has trimmed it down to a 15-second pitch!

Call it what you want, this thing will change the way you market yourself and your music and give everyone some context to understand what you do. It is critical that you have a concise and easy-to-understand pitch that will help you shape your brand.

Your pitch does not have to be lengthy to be effective; it just has to explain your sound in a few words or sentences.

Here are some of my clients' best pitches to jump-start your brain:

The Divorcees – The hard liquor sandwich of Americana: 1 shot each of Jager (Cash), Tequila (Willie) and Whiskey (Waylon)

Leftover Salmon – Polyethnic Cajun Slamgrass

John Taglieri – If Vertical Horizon and Third Eye Blind got hit by Train!

Devil Doll – Jessica Rabbit meets Joan Jett

Bamboo Shoots – Prince making out with INXS in the bathroom of CBGBs.

WATCH THE PERFECT PITCH VIDEO

Here is a video of me and Derek Sivers talking about how to craft the perfect pitch: http://www.tinyurl.com/PitchDerek

CREATING YOUR PITCH

First, take a deep breath, clear your head, and tell yourself that what you are about to do is exactly like writing a song.

You do not record the first thing that comes out (or at least I hope you don't, but that's a different conversation). It takes some honing and some tweaking and possibly some collaboration.

It's the same process to create your perfect pitch.

STEP ONE: WRITE DOWN THE FOLLOWING:

1. Genres you play: Roots, rock, reggae, folk, punk, jazz, alt-country, chillout, funk, etc.

(No more than two or three will actually be selected in the end).

2. Write all the artists that other people say you sound like.

3. Write a list of all artists (or authors or famous people) that have influenced you.

4. Write down all of the feelings and vibes that you want to create or convey with your music.

STEP TWO: CHOOSE YOUR FAVORITES

Now look back at your notes and use these elements as a guideline to help you come up with a few words or sentences that sum you up.

Circle the ones that resonate the most for you.

STEP THREE: LOG ON AND TEST IT OUT

Go to this fabulous website:

http://www.15secondpitch.com

This website will help you structure and hone your pitch, and it will TIME you, too!

(This site is a business pitch site, but you ARE a business and the structure that it provides is very helpful.)

> **TIP:** By using this site you will show up on the first page of Google when you enter your profile here – this will help you get found online and in search engines.

STEP FOUR: WRITE OUT YOUR PITCH HERE:

Read it out loud standing in front of the mirror.

Do you love it?

If you don't, then don't use it.

I once worked with a band that chose the term "Soul Rock" to describe their sound. After it was published countless times they were hating it, so make sure your pitch is something that you can deal with in print over and over again, and that it's something you won't get sick of.

STEP FIVE: SAY IT OUT LOUD

Now stand in front of the mirror and practice saying it out loud.

Does it feel comfortable to say it?

If you feel like you're speaking your truth, you will absolutely know, and then it is the perfect pitch for you.

Still not sure? Read it to a bunch of friends and fans and ask them to work on it with you. Don't overthink it. Keep it as simple and as concise as you can.

STEP SIX: PLACE YOUR PITCH

Now that you have it, you're going to place it in the following places.

What you are doing now is branding yourself.

Online Branding:

1. On your website's homepage (yes, on the HOMEPAGE, and on as many pages as you can: at the top of your bio, and on any page your fans may land on – not buried in the site)

2. On your MySpace page

3. On your Twitter page – in the area that says "bio"

4. On your Facebook page – in the area that says "profile"

5. On all other social networking sites and anywhere else you have an online presence

Offline Branding:

1. On your postcards

2. On your show flyers

3. On your business cards

4. On your posters

5. On anything else you have in print

So now when you're out somewhere and you hand someone a flyer announcing your show, you're handing someone your brand.

People will know exactly what you do, and it will be truly effective marketing.

Not sure if you've hit the nail on the head?

FREE PITCH ANALYSIS

This book comes with a membership to to my private online Mastermind Group.

To get signed up, email Contact@ArielPublicity.com with the subject line **"I bought the book!"** and you will receive a link to sign up.

Once you do, fill out your profile and send your pitch to the forum, and I or one of the site administrators will give you honest feedback, and so will the whole group.

NOTES

WEEK 3: OPTIMIZING YOUR WEBSITE

This week's lesson is about optimizing your website and setting it up so that it does two critical things: 1) serves as a vehicle for building your email list and 2) helps you create two-way communication between you and your fans. This will in the end make you more money.

Social Media is all about two-way conversations – not just having a static website packed with unchanging brochure-like material. You want an interactive and engaging website that pulls people in at first and makes them want to come back often and interact with you.

Your website should do 2 things:

1. Help you build your list

2. Make you $$$

6 SURE-FIRE WAYS TO CATCH & HOLD YOUR FAN BASE

Follow these rules and start getting casual visitors to become fans.

1. Add Your Pitch to Your Homepage

Last week you created it and by now you should have already added your pitch to your homepage and anywhere else you have an online presence: MySpace, Twitter, Facebook, etc.

If you have not done this already, please go back and handle this important step before you move ahead with this module.

2. Your Site Must Load in LESS than 3.5 Seconds

Recent studies show that people have the attention span of gnats and that if they have to wait more than 3.5 seconds for a site to load, they're moving on to another site. So, time your site and make sure it loads in less than 3.5 seconds.

3. NO Flash Intros

Flash intros are popular, but I urge you to skip the temptation to have one! You want to have a clean, easy-to-load page that instantly connects you and your information directly to your fans. A Flash intro is unreadable to search engines, meaning you will not be findable in Google, which is critical to your online strategy and your online success. I've heard that the newest version of Flash actually is readable by search engines but I suggest you skip it all together.

4. Have a Consistent Look and Feel and Name All Over the Net

Your site should have the same color scheme and theme throughout ALL of the pages so that visitors do not think they have landed on another site while surfing through yours. Studies show that when people feel uncomfortable online they move on – and they feel uncomfortable when the consistency changes. The same goes for Social Networking sites; make sure your MySpace and Twitter themes match your website – if your website is blue, your MySpace and Twitter pages should also be blue. Also, use the same handle wherever possible: you.com should match your myspace.com/you and your Twitter/you.

5. Give Away an Exclusive, Free MP3 / Video to Satisfy the WIIFM – What's In It For Me? (your fan's little voice)

Every consumer (read: fan) on earth, when confronted with the option to buy something is thinking: WIIFM? *What's In It For Me* is driving your fans at all times. Therefore, you must offer them something they can't refuse.

People can't refuse free stuff – so offer free stuff on your homepage!

You must create a bribe on your homepage to encourage people to sign up to your email list, which should be prominently highlighted on your homepage.

This bribe should be exclusive only to your homepage, and should not be available anywhere else online.

This free offering is a gift that people receive when they sign up for your monthly newsletter; it's your way of saying, "Thank you for being my fan!"

DO NOT put a box on your page saying ,"Join Our Email List." What this is conveying is: "Hey fan sign up for our email list so we can send you more email." Instead, make an offer that they can't refuse. Word it in a way that answers the WIIFM (What's In It For Me) question. I recommend saying, "Sign Up For Our Monthly Newsletter List and Receive Exclusive MP3s Every Single Month," or "Sign Up For Our Mailing List and Receive a Free Download Instantly."

> **TIP:** Your webmaster should be able to program this easily. If you don't have a webmaster that can handle this, I suggest the ReverbNation widget called "Exclusive Downloads". You can find it here: http://www.tinyurl.com/ReverbFreeBribe To install it on your Facebook or MySpace, just follow directions on the Reverb Nation site.

6. Make It Clear and Set Them at Ease

You want to make sure that it is very obvious to your visitors that the moment they sign up on your mailing list they will be receiving their free MP3 or video, and that they're also getting signed up for your newsletter.

Also, on your homepage, you should put in small letters: "We will never sell, rent or lend your email addresses to anyone else ever," so that people can be assured that their email addresses are safe with you.

TIP: It is NOT COOL (actually it may be illegal) to sign people up to your email list without their permission, so make sure you ask if its OK before you sign anyone up to receive your newsletter. You do not want to be reported as a spammer.

NOTES

WEEK 4: SOCIAL MEDIA FOR MUSICIANS

PART 1 - WEB 2.0 DEFINED

So, you probably have heard people using the term Web 2.0 and you may not have known what they were talking about. It's an important principle to grasp before we dive into Social Media sites as they all operate in a Web 2.0 environment.

WEB 1.0 VS. WEB 2.0 - A QUICK SUMMARY

Web 1.0 is the Internet that we all grew up on where websites are mostly informational "brochure-like" or "static" sites with the same basic information included on each one: Homepage, About, Bio, Mission, Buy, Contact Us, etc.

In Web 1.0, you surf to each portal and check it out passively. You can find out a lot of information about whatever you are looking for on a site like this, but it's a one-way conversation from the creator of the site to you (the customer).

Web 2.0 (referring to the second generation of Internet-based services) is just a fancy term for the ongoing transition of the web from a collection of static websites to a more interactive platform.

Its main features include:

• Social networking sites (MySpace, Facebook, YouTube, Twitter)

• User contributed sites (wikis, wikipedia)

• Self-publishing platforms (blogs, podcasts, vlogs, vodcasts)

• Tagging & social bookmarking (Delicious, Digg)

Web 2.0 Is Made Possible By 2 Things:

• New programming languages allowing more interactivity, which were not around when the web first started to gain popularity

• The widespread availability of broadband

In other words, Web 2.0 is interactive and social – it requires participation. In Web 2.0, users share and contribute ideas and content... and that content can spread virally (think YouTube videos we have all seen). And finally, Web 2.0 is about being *all over the net* – it is no longer acceptable to be just in one place (that's 1.0 thinking).

WATERING YOUR SOCIAL MEDIA GARDEN

One thing to keep in mind is that Social Media is much like a garden. It takes consistent cultivation and weeding to make it thrive. Just planting once and leaving it alone will not make your garden grow. Joining multiple networks will help you spread your word and connect with others. Once you participate in a two-way conversation, you will get support from other users on these sites.

Each Web 2.0 environment has its own protocol that you must follow. As you get to know the rules, you will start to reap the benefits of tying into each community.

The #1 complaint that I get from artists is they do not want to get involved with multiple websites. It's just too much, they don't have time, and they don't like it!

I understand your feelings, and I sympathize – however, you will be left behind in the dust to die in obscurity if you cannot change with the times. In order to be on the court as an artist you must participate in the game and you must be on at least a few sites.

I will outline the sites that I think are critical to get you started, in the order that I suggest diving in.

The following list may feel a bit overwhelming – deep breath! My suggestion is that if you are in a band, get one member to each take a site / task.

GETTING STARTED – UNDERSTANDING WEB 2.0 IN LESS THAN 15 MINUTES

Before you attempt to dive into this new and complex world, I highly recommend that you spend 15 minutes at this website:

http://www.commoncraft.com

This site has produced a few short movies that will explain the basic terms of Web 2.0 and Social Media in plain English.

These videos are short and they are brilliant. I suggest you start with these and I will reference others throughout this book.

1. Social Networking in Plain English:
    http://www.commoncraft.com/video-social-networking

2. Social Media in Plain English:
    http://www.commoncraft.com/socialmedia

3. Social Bookmarking in Plain English:
    http://www.commoncraft.com/bookmarking-plain-english

4. Wikis in Plain English:
    http://www.commoncraft.com/video-wikis-plain-english

WIDGETS

Another common Web 2.0 tool you will see are widgets. I'm going to be referring to "widgets" in the coming chapters of this book. A widget (sometimes called a badge) is simply a small piece of code that you can copy and paste into the HTML (programming) of any site and when you update a widget in one place it updates all over the web. You can put the same widget on MySpace,

Facebook, and your own Blog, update it once and it will be updated all over the internet. My favorite widgets are available at http://www.ReverbNation.com

PART 2: SOCIAL MEDIA MUST-HAVES – TWITTER, FACEBOOK, FLICKR & PODCASTS

Twitter only takes a few minutes to sign up for, so we are going to start with it first.

TWITTER

Twitter is an ingenious solution that will give your fans more of you, connect you to conversations with people, and it takes less than 3 minutes a day to use effectively – without your computer –and it can be synched to Facebook to double its effectiveness!

The Twitter site says: "Twitter is for staying in touch and keeping up with friends no matter where you are or what you're doing."

First – Watch These Videos:

Twitter in Plain English:
http://www.commoncraft.com/twitter

Twitter Search in Plain English:
http://www.commoncraft.com/twitter-search

Five Reasons Why You, My Dear Musician, Should Care About Twitter:

1. Twitter is free and very easy to join!

2. Twitter will help you build your brand, and it's much easier to stay current with than a blog, because all you need to do is "tweet" small texts (the 140 character limit ensures that you won't blather on forever).

3. Twitter makes your fan base feel more connected to you, like they are interacting directly with you. And, bonus: you don't have to follow everyone who follows you.

4. Twitter is an amazing way to quickly join specific conversations based on topics or locations.

5. Twitter gives you customizable and cool "badges ", which are widgets that you can drop onto your website and your MySpace page (as well as onto your blog and your Reverb Nation page), so your fans can follow you from your multiple platforms.

Step 1: Think About Your Brand First

Set up an account—use your full name, or your band name, whatever name it is that you want people to be able to find using Google. This is very important. Don't just pick a name you like. Whatever name you choose on Twitter becomes Google-able. Choose something you're comfortable with, that you want to do well in search results, and that's the name you want to get out there.

Step 2: Sign Up

Go to http://www.twitter.com

Twitter will take you through a few sign-up steps and you will enter or create your username, password, and register your e-mail.

Twitter will search your e-mail address book to see if anyone you know is already on it. You may be surprised at just how many people you know are already using it. You will also have the option of sending email invites to your friends.

> **TIP:** Take some time and set up your profile properly. You probably had a Website made for your music and that involved spending money. You put a lot of thought into it. Here's a chance to have a free Website. Put up a good profile picture. That's the little, tiny square picture that goes next to all your messages. Add your pitch and link to your Web page in your profile, under the Bio section.

Step 3: Link Your Mobile

You should enter your cell phone number if you want to accept tweets via text. This will depend on your text-messaging plan and your tolerance for receiving multiple texts. You will have the option to receive tweets to your phone from selected individuals, so you can have only a few people tweet straight to your phone.

> **TIP:** To text from your mobile phone from the USA send messages to **40404** and they will immediately go to your Twitter feed, or use an app like Tweetdeck or Tweetie (iPhone) or UberTwitter & SocialScope (Blackberry)

> **TIP:** To message friends who follow you from your cell phone, you can type "d" (for direct) then their username. This is very useful when you are out and about and you don't have their mobile phone numbers and it's a great way to avoid roaming charges for friends out of the country.

Step 4: Search Keywords

Next, go to the search page: http://www.search.twitter.com. On this page, start searching keywords – words that are important to you, topics that you like to write about, words about the music you play, whether it be the genre or the instrument. That gives you a jumping-off point.

Step 5: Link Twitter to Update Your Facebook Status

Next go to http://tinyurl.com/TwitterTweetFB and you can link your Twitter page directly to your Facebook page. You will be able to update your status on Facebook by using Twitter from your phone.

Step 6: Share Photos With Twitpic

Sign up using your Twitter username and password and start sharing images from your phone. http://twitpic.com/

Step 7: Follow Lots of People

Twitter does not work in a vacuum, so the key is to follow at least 100 people!

I interviewed Laura Fitton, one of the authors of Twitter For Dummies, and there is an in-depth article on this subject that includes a list of some people in the music business to check out and follow here: http://tinyurl.com/TwitterAriel.

EXERCISE:
MAKE YOUR TWITTER MATCH YOUR BRAND

Start a Twitter Account for your band

I also suggest registering your first and last name so you will have 2 accounts – one can re-direct to the other (to see what I mean go to http://www.twitter.com/arielhyatt).

If you already have a Twitter Account make sure you follow these steps:

Step 1: Add your pitch as your description, with a link back to your website and an offer to sign up to your newsletter list.

Step 2: Make sure your background profile colors match your MySpace colors, and your photo matches your main image on your website (a logo can stand out even more than a photo).

Step 3: Make sure you are following at least 100 people (including me, please: http://www.twitter.com/cyberpr).

Step 4: Post to the closed Mastermind site so we can all follow and support each other.

Step 5: Please post other suggestions for who to follow as well!

Step 6: Use these great tools to manage Twitter easily from your Desktop or PDA mobile: http://tweetdeck.com.

For iPhones: I suggest Tweetie and Tweetdeck – available at the app store for download.

For Blackberrys: Download Twitterberry - http://tinyurl.com/GetBerry

FACEBOOK

100 million people log in to Facebook everyday. You won't believe how many people who you never saw around MySpace are on Facebook. All of a sudden you will be back in touch with your babysitter from grade school, a ton of old friends, and even the drummer from your first band. And, if you have been resisting because you think Facebook is just for kids in college, you are mistaken. The largest demographic on Facebook is people over 35. It's the 4th most-trafficked website in the world, and it's the number one photo-sharing application.

Facebook has over 200 million active users. It's here to stay, so my advice is dive in (if you haven't already).

Here is a quick rundown for newbies on how to create a page as a band/musician, plus my favorite apps for musicians when pimping out your Facebook profile!

FACEBOOK FOR NEWBIES—HOW TO SET UP A PROFILE

Step 1: Create a Band/Artist Profile. Go to:
http://www.new.facebook.com/pages/create.php

Step 2: Click on the third button down, it will say: Artist, Band, or Public Figure.

Step 3: Select Band or Musician. After you select it, a pull-down menu will pop up. Select band if you are a band, or musician if you play solo or want to create a solo page (you can create as many as you want, so you can create one for you and one for your band).

Step 4: Enter your name. Name your page and select Create Page. You are now off to the races!

The rest is pretty self-explanatory: You upload your photo for your main user icon, your bio, band members and photos and details.

Step 5: Click Create Page. Now you are live and ready to add Apps! What is an App? It's short for application, and it is simply a cool additional tool that you can add to your page so that you can display features such as music, photos, and videos.

Facebook has a great page that helps you with apps in the FAQ's.

ARIEL'S TOP FACEBOOK APPS FOR MUSICIANS

Here are my top picks for musicians and links to where you can download the apps for your own profile.

1. My Band by ReverbNation

http://tinyurl.com/FacebookMyBand

Post unlimited songs for streaming or download, add bios and photos, sell music and tickets, and grow your mailing list. You can also have your friends add your music and share it with their friends (viral marketing for you!)

2. Flickr to Facebook

http://tinyurl.com/Flickr2Facebook

You can synch both sites instantly – follow the directions and moving ahead you will upload your photos to Flickr and they will instantly post to Facebook as well. We will be covering Flickr in the next section.

I am a big advocate of creating small casual videos to share with your fans. Videos are an excellent viral-marketing tool. This app is the easiest way to show your videos that are already loaded onto YouTube.

3. Twitter – Tweet Away and Have It Synched!

http://tinyurl.com/TwitterTweetFB

This app allows you to update your status on Facebook straight from your mobile phone. So you can be on the road but your Facebook page can be updated from your van! Pretty cool, eh?

4. Selective Twitter

http://tinyurl.com/SelectiveTweet

Selective Twitter Status lets you update your Facebook status from Twitter – but you can choose which tweets you want.

Just end each tweet with #fb when you want to post it as your Facebook status. This is amazing, because you can update your personal page OR your band page, depending on how you feel and what you want to share that day!

5. Facebook Mobile

http://www.facebook.com/mobile

This app allows you to use Facebook on the go. With it, you can quickly to upload photos and notes from your camera phone straight to Facebook. You can also receive and reply to Facebook messages, pokes and Wall posts using text messages, or use your phone's mobile browser.

6. YouTube

http://tinyurl.com/Facebook2Youtube

Share your favorite videos on your profile and pages. Easily find videos, add them to your favorites and share with friends. It will also synchronize with your YouTube account.

7. Music Powered By iLike

http://tinyurl.com/FacebookiLikeApp

Create an artist page, upload your music and events. This app also lets you send multimedia bulletins to fans and get detailed statistics.

Happy Facebooking and please find me and join our group which features loads of free tips for musicians:

http://www.facebook.com/CyberPR

FLICKR:
YOUR VISUAL PHOTOBLOG

Are you too lazy to blog? Does blogging feel like a huge, annoying, and daunting task that is evocative of being a kid again and getting a huge homework assignment?

Well, fear not. I've got a great and easy blogging solution –

http://www.flickr.com

First – Watch the video

Photo Sharing in Plain English:

http://www.commoncraft.com/photosharing

They say a picture says a thousand words, and it's true.

Flickr is one of the user-friendliest Web 2.0 sites, and Yahoo owns it, so millions of potential new fans are waiting for you to discover them and make friends. Flickr works in many ways just like MySpace or Facebook. You create a profile, upload your main image, join groups, and make friends. You can also direct-message people and leave comments on any photo you like.

PHOTOS TELL A COMPLETE STORY OF YOU!

On Flickr you can post photos of things other than your band activities – such as vacations, kids, your home, and hobbies to show your fans you are a well-rounded individual. If you go to conferences, this is a great way to connect with people you meet (remember, the most interesting thing for people is themselves).

Create A VIP Photo-Sharing Experience For Your Fans

Your photos can be marked "private" so only approved fans and friends can see certain photos. Flickr lets you choose which sets to share. I suggest creating a VIP area of fun / special photos that only gives access to your registered fans / friends / street team as an added bonus for them to link to you.

TOP 10 REASONS WHY MUSICIANS SHOULD USE FLICKR

1. *The #1 Reason:* It Helps You Build Your Fan Base. One of the best things about Flickr is that you can search to join groups and make new friends, fans and contacts.

2. *It's Easy.* If blogging overwhelms you with all of the writing, Flickr is a perfect choice. All you need to do is upload photos from your cell phone or digital camera, create brief captions and tag things properly and voilà!

3. *Make A Personal Connection With Your Fans.* It's a great way for them to see other dimensions of you and get "behind the scenes."

4. *You Can Create Multiple Photo Sets* – break them up by categories within your site, so people who are interested in live music could go to your live shots, people who are interested in candid shots of the band having fun can go to those shots, etc.

5. *Start Your Own Flickr Group & Get Known.* In addition to your personal page, you can start a group and invite others to join. Groups could be for "backstage shots" or "on-the-road photos" or "musicians and their dogs"– get creative – start a new community that no one has thought of yet. You can also join Flickr groups and network with others by leaving comments on their photos.

6. *Create Sets That Will Drive Traffic By Linking To Other Groups.* Examples include Music festivals, Live Shots, Fan shots etc. –I included a list to get you started later in this chapter.

7. *Use Flickr To Promote Your Own Site.* As people come and browse your photos, include links to your site to drive traffic to you.

8. *Create Cool Digital Postcards To Send To Your Fans.* Flickr has a wonderful sister site called Delivr that allows you to send any of your photos as a postcard: http://www.delivr.net

9. *Flickr Connects Directly To Your Facebook Page.* You can synch both sites instantly – follow these directions: http://tinyurl.com/Flickr2Facebook

10. *Get The Cutest / Coolest Business Cards On Earth.* Flickr works with a site called Moo and they make the greatest cards with assorted photos on each – a cool and creative way to share your info: http://www.moo.com/flickr

SOME PHOTO SET IDEAS

Here are some ideas for grouping your newly uploaded photos:

Fans in The Audience – You can create a whole album of just fans by taking pictures of fans at your shows. Your fans are interested in themselves (and each other) as well as you and your music!

Posed Shots Of Fans – Ask your fans who are loyal followers to send in great photos of themselves with captions they create. This will keep your fans coming back to see themselves.

Food – Take photos of all the food you eat on the road or take a picture of your lunch every day and make a photo plates diary.

Behind The Scenes – Take pictures of you in the studio, loading your gear into a club, writing music, buying instruments, etc., and add comments about what the life of a musician is from behind the scenes.

Band Candids – Outtakes from photo shoots and videos. Live shots.

Music Festivals / Conferences – When you go to CMJ, SXSW etc. you can maximize your experience by covering all events. Many of these music festivals have their own Flickr sites so you can upload those photo sets directly to each Flickr group and use them to network with the people that were there.

TIP: How to add a contact: Simply click on the image of the person (the Buddy Icon) you want to add and a menu will pop up and direct you! Loads of questions can be answered here if you get stuck: http://www.flickr.com/help/faq

Some Flickr Groups to Check Out & Join:

Ariel Publicity & Cyber PR – Be Our Friend!

http://www.flickr.com/photos/ArielPublicityPR

Band Publicity Photos:

http://tinyurl.com/FlickrBandShot

Music Directory:

http://www.flickr.com/groups/MusicDirectory

Girls With Guitars:

http://www.flickr.com/groups/GirlsWithGuitars

Music Makers:

http://www.flickr.com/groups/MusicMakers

My Love Affair With Music:

http://www.flickr.com/groups/MusicLovers/

Live Music Photography:

http://tinyurl.com/FlickrLiveMusic

Live Music:

http://www.flickr.com/groups/Live-Music/

I'd love to join your groups and see your photos, so please do include me as a friend once you get started. I can be found at http://www.flickr.com/ArielPublicityPR

PODCASTS

Okay, let's start with another great movie!

http://commoncraft.com/podcasting

The fastest way to get involved with Podcasting is to join **Music Alley** from Mevio (which used to be known as the Podsafe Music Network).

When you become a podsafe artist you are allowing podcasters to use your tracks in their shows without worrying about clearance issues. This means you are giving away your tracks for them to use royalty-free, in exchange for podcast play and promotion.

I am a huge fan and advocate of podcasting, and the podcasting community is both tight-knit and wonderful.

Hundreds of podcasters use **Music Alley** to get music for their podcasts, and the bonus is you can see who is logging in, choosing your music, and adding it to their podcasts.

TO JOIN MUSIC ALLEY:

Step 1: Sign Up

Go to http://music.mevio.com and click on the green box that says: Artists submit your music and watch your fans and CD sales grow.

Step 2: Complete the Artist Registration Form

You will create a username and a password for yourself here and use this in the future to check which podcasters are including you on their shows.

Step 3: Monitor Your Podcast Plays

When you get played there will be a link to the podcast to check out!

I highly suggest that you log on and listen to the podcast so you can hear yourself and hear what the podcaster had to say about you. The only way to forge authentic relationships with podcasters is by listening to their shows.

HOW TO THANK A PODCASTER WHO PLAYS YOUR MUSIC

Podcasters are hobbyists who work very hard to create fun and quality podcasts because they love music. The BEST thing you can do to ingratiate yourself with this community is to thank them for including you. They will love you for this and play more of your music in the future

1. Record a Custom Station ID as a Thank You.

Create an MP3 with the podcast name.

The script can be creative but should include the following key points:

"Hey, this is (Band / Artist Name) and you're listening to our new record (Album Title) on (name of podcast). Check us out at (Band Website / MySpace page)."

The more creative the better, play music, make funny voices etc. but try to keep it under 20 seconds.

2. Acknowledge the Creator of The Podcast By Doing One of the Following:

i.   Twitter about the podcast with a link to it.

ii. Blog about the podcast in your MySpace or website blog.

iii. Post the link and a thank you to your status updates on Facebook.

iv. Leave a message on the podcasters VM thanking them for the add. (Many podcasters have telephone #s listed on their sites with answering machines hooked up to them where you can leave a message – most of the time they will play the message on another podcast and also add another song to their playlist, so this is very beneficial!)

v.   Add a link back to their site on your website or on your blogroll.

vi. Review the podcast on iTunes – this is the BEST way to thank a podcaster as well-reviewed podcasts move up the charts at iTunes.

NOTES

WEEK 5: BLOGGING

In the first edition of this book, Blogging was part of the chapter on Social Media – but it is such an involved topic that it now has its own chapter. Before you dive in, I highly suggest that you read this entire chapter first and try to get familiar with the blogging world by reading blogs to get the lay of the land. After a few days of reading, you can begin posting comments on blogs you like.

Intro - Movie Time!

RSS in Plain English:
http://www.commoncraft.com/rss_plain_english

Blogs in Plain English:
http://www.commoncraft.com/blogs

GETTING PREPARED TO MANAGE BLOG READING

CREATE YOUR GOOGLE RSS READER

Now you know exactly what this is from watching RSS in Plain English. Setting up your RSS Reader is the perfect way to get the information you want (not only from blogs but also from other sites you frequently visit) to come to you, instead of having to check constantly to see what has been updated.

CREATE YOUR BLOG READER PROFILES

Blog Reader Profiles are wonderful because they will show the blogger and the reader community that you have visited a blog even if you do not choose to comment each and everytime. This leaves a trail of breadcrumbs leading back to you, which shows others what you are interested in.

So, if you visit a blog that has either My Blog Log or Google Friend Connect installed, a photo of you / your band logo will show up on the blog you visited. This is a great way of becoming extra-memorable to bloggers. Each of these takes just a few minutes to set up:

MY BLOG LOG

http://www.mybloglog.com

Look for the green tab at the top of the page that says "join/sign in" and fill out your profile.

GOOGLE FRIEND CONNECT

http://www.google.com/friendconnect

When you get to this site, press the blue "get started" button and set up your profile. Add your photo, short bio, and links to your website, Facebook, Myspace and Twitter.

CHOOSE A FEW BLOGS TO GET STARTED

According to some statistics there are currently over 80 million active bloggers today. Blogs, as you know, can be about any topic. A few dozen people read some blogs, while some are read by millions. The vast majority of all bloggers create blogs for no financial gain whatsoever; in fact it usually costs music bloggers money to host their files and maintain their blogs. A blog is usually a private endeavor. Most bloggers create their blogs as a personal outlet where they can talk about their lives, their opinions, the things that they like and dislike – it's basically an online diary.

To find blogs that are right for you won't take long – just dive in and start reading them. The ones that resonate will jump out at you.

HOW TO GET REVIEWED ON BLOGS – A STEP-BY-STEP GUIDE

A fascinating study from NYU's Stern Business School came out in 2007. This study was based on the correlation of album sales and blog posts, and the researchers discovered the following:

- If 40 or more blog posts were made before an album's release, sales ended up being three to four times the average, for both independent and major label releases

- If blog posts crossed 250, album sales rose to six times the average regardless of label

Full report here:

http://tinyurl.com/NYUblog

This is HUGE NEWS. For the past few years everyone in the music business has been scratching their heads and asking: How do we sell more records?

Blogs are the answer! (and academically researched no less)

So, what does this mean for you?

It means it's time to get your album blogged about!

As a recovered traditional publicist with a background in writing press releases, announcing things, and blatantly pitching my clients, I had to relearn from scratch everything I thought I knew about how to promote music when I started to approach bloggers.

Bloggers are a quirky lot. I know this, because I've spent the last couple of years observing bloggers, interacting with bloggers through my business, and attending some of the most notable blog conferences on earth.

So, how on earth are you supposed to interrupt and say: *"Hey blogger, come write about me in your personal diary!?"*

There are a few ways to do this. Here are your options:

OPTION #1: START YOUR OWN BLOG

My number one piece of advice if you're trying to get known in the blogosphere is: do like they do. Start your own blog. This is a good idea for many reasons aside from attracting other bloggers. If you don't know the big secret already: Bloggers read other bloggers' blogs!

But aside from this, having your own blog has many benefits for you as an artist:

Top 9 Reasons Every Musician Should Blog

1. A blog allows your fans to get more of you.

2. A blog allows fans to go backstage, into your life and see sides of you they may not know about.

3. A blog is a great way to create fresh new content aside from recording music.

4. A blog encourages a two-way conversation between you and your fans.

5. Fans can subscribe to your blog using an RSS reader and get new updates sent directly to them without having to visit your site over and over.

6. You can syndicate your blog all over the Internet: MySpace, Reverb Nation, Facebook, Twitter, Flickr and your own site are just a few places where people may encounter it.

7. Blog posts are indexed in Google making topics you choose to write about findable. This could bring you more fans who were not out to hear your music but are interested in whatever your blog posts are about and become fans as a result.

8. Other bloggers are more likely to read your blog and post comments – a sure fire way of getting mentioned on even more blogs.

9. You can add other bloggers who acknowledge your blog onto your blogroll – this is critical in blog world to associate yourself with other blogs and communities of people that you would like to connect with and who will want to connect with you.

You don't have to only blog about your music – you can talk about your home life, your TV habit, your favorite foods, your day job, your fitness routine – anything! The key here is that you must post regularly and consistently. If you are in a band, having each band member contribute one post a month is a great way to keep new content flowing.

TIP: Don't overthink! Just post! I know how musicians can be. Do not treat this like a rehearsal or think you have to make every sentence perfect. The point of a blog is that it is an informal endeavor. Just get posting, don't stress about it and tweak it to death. (I would, however, recommend spell check).

A lot of artists ask me if they can hire someone to blog for them – I do not recommend this. People will see right through this if posts are not coming from you (unless you make it EXTREMELY transparent like – "notes from our biggest fan," or "road diary from our tour manager").

TIP: You cannot have someone blog as you (tempting right?) – this is something you must undertake. To be part of social networking, you must participate.

How to Set Up a Blog:

I'm not going to go into the details about how to set them up because you can easily find guides on how to do this via Google but both of these sites are wonderful, and you can get going within minutes of signing up:

http://www.Blogger.com

http://www.Wordpress.com

For a more advanced approach I would suggest hiring a web designer to install a Wordpress blog right onto your website. This should not cost you more than a few hundred dollars and your blog will then be integrated into your site. I suggest that you add /blog to your personal URL. For example, my blog can be found at

http://arielpublicity.com/blog

> **TIP:** My web design firm would be happy to help you. Contact Bob Stovern at http://thedigitalbob.com

> **TIP:** If you have a website hosted by Hostbaby, they will set up your Wordpress blog for you. Contact hostbaby@hostbaby.com – I highly suggest this route because then your blog will be in the same place as your website and not on a Blogger or Wordpress site.

WRITTEN EXERCISE: YOUR 50 BLOG TARGETS

(This one requires your trusty notebook AND a computer… or skip the notebook and just bookmark your 50 targets online)

Identify 50 blogs where you want to be reviewed.

Once you have your own blog up and running (if you are intimidated by this part, skip it – you can still get results), the next step is to identify which blogs you would like to be included on – and then to start reading them and posting comments on them.

Remember, the NYU study shows that if 40 or more blog posts were made before an album's release, sales ended up being three to four times as high.

If you don't know how to search for blogs, here is a way to get started. Search blogs using these search engines:

www.blogsearch.google.com

http://www.technorati.com

http://hypem.com

> **TIP:** Start with one blog that you like and then look at the blogroll (a list of other blogs it links to) to lead you to other blogs to check out.

1.

2.

3.

4.

5.

6.

7.

8.

9.

10.

11.

12.

13.

14.

15.

16.

17.

18.

19.

20.

 21.

22.

23.

24.

25.

26.

27.

28.

29.

30.

31

32.

33.

34.

35.

36.

37.

38.

39.

40.

41.

42.

43.

44.

45.

46.

47.

48.

49.

50.

Add These 50 targets to Your Blogroll!

> **TIP:** The NYU study showed that some of these blogs should be the bigger and more widely read blogs like Pitchfork and BrooklynVegan. These are great targets, but I suggest you target blogs that are more likely to cover you based on what they are already writing about. The most popular music blogs that everyone constantly mentions tend to be indie-rock centric, so if you do not play indie rock then you may not have a chance of getting included.

And be sure to do an Internet search to see if anyone has written about you on a blog already. With 80 million blogs out there, it's possible you have been mentioned somewhere and not even know it.

If you find a post, PERFECT! Post a comment back thanking them for their post and say something about their blog – the idea here is create a two-way conversation by talking about THEM. Use a sig file identifying yourself so they know where to visit you online.

Here's what my sig file looks like:

Ariel Hyatt

CYBER PR

Digital Campaigns for Musicians, Filmmakers & Authors

Ariel@ArielPublicity.com

http://www.arielpublicity.com/blog

http://Twitter.com/CyberPR

> **TIP:** Add the blogs that mention you to your blogroll. A blogroll is simply a list that links to other blogs. You see them on every single blog you go to (they are the big lists of other blogs and sites in the margin of the blog).

> **TIP:** Remember, comments should never be self-promotional. At first, they should be entirely about the blog and the blogger. Post comments, comment on how you like their blog. Add feedback. Disagree, agree… but participate in the blog. When you are a blogger, it's all about how many comments you have and how many people you are engaging on your blog. This part is critical.

WRITTEN EXCERCISE: BLOG TOPIC LOCATOR - ARTISTS YOU KNOW / PLAY WITH

If you do not find any posts about your music, a great way to start is to search blogs for other artists you know and/ or play with.

Write the names of 5–10 artists that you know and play with here that match your genre.

1.

2.

3.

4.

5.

6.

7.

8.

9.

10.

Now, you can reach out with a personal note (or comment) and say something like:

> "I just read your post about Elizabeth and The Catapult. I couldn't agree with you more, they put on a great live show. In fact we played with them just a few months ago and I was blown away etc."

Say something very specific about their blog post and then add your own detailed comments. Keep in mind that blogs are all about adding to the community, so be a contribution.

> **TIP:** Don't ask for a review on your first contact with a blogger – just make an observation about them and comment on what they are writing. There will be plenty of time to make yourself known later – this is a process that takes some time.

Remember, bloggers are people too, and all PR is about connecting personally. If you do not handle this tactfully, the blogger will sense that you are just trying to get something.

SEARCH BY SOUND ALIKE & COMPARISON

Another way to identify appropriate blogs is to look for posts about bands that you get compared to and that you sound like.

> **TIP:** Stay away from the huge names like Bob Dylan and search for more niche artists you get compared to.

The next thing to do is to visit these blogs and take a peek. Is this the kind of the blog that would write about you and your music? If so, add this blog to your RSS Reader, and then return to comment on this blog often. Add this blog to your blogroll, so that the blogger can see you are visiting their blog often, and start posting comments.

> **TIP:** In order to become sticky you will have to post comments on other people's blogs regularly and get to be known by the blogger before you make your first pitch.

After a few weeks of tracking and posting, you could write a simple hello to the blogger, mention that you have a blog, and some music that you would like them to check out, and then subtly see if you can encourage them to check out your music.

After you get your first review, remember to link back to your blog and thank the blogger.

Like I said before, bloggers read other bloggers' blogs. Soon, you will begin to spread around the net.

OPTION #2: BECOME AN AVID BLOG READER & COMMENT BACK

Option #2 is a bit less time consuming because you will not have to build and maintain your own blog, but you will still have to create personal relationships with bloggers. If you are going to go this route, I suggest you build a links page on your website or feature bloggers on your top friends on your MySpace page, or become friends with them on Facebook. You must acknowledge other blogs so that you are still somewhat in the two-way conversation which is critical.

Follow all the steps above but skip the "create your own blog" part.

OPTION #3: HIRE A SOCIAL MEDIA PR FIRM TO HANDLE BLOG PLACEMENTS FOR YOU

I suggest that you do your research thoroughly and make sure you are very clear what it is you want before you go down this path.

There is a guide I wrote called "The Musicians Guide To Choosing The Perfect Publicist" and it is in the bonus chapter of this book. Read it before you hire someone! Or, better yet hire me. Information and Cyber PR rates can be found at http://www.cyberprmusic.com

OPTION #4: ATTEND CONFERENCES AND MEET-UPS AND MEET BLOGGERS FACE TO FACE

This is a great way to get into the blogging community. This is how Tim Ferris launched his wildly successful book *The 4 Hour Work Week*. I can't confirm this, but it makes perfect sense.

Here are a few I suggest:

SXSW Interactive

http://www.SXSW.com

Mid-March in Austin, TX.

• BlogHer

http://www.blogher.com/topic/blogher-conferences

July in San Francisco, CA.

• Blog World Expo

http://www.newmediaexpo.com

October in Las Vegas, NV.

• Gnomedex

http://www.gnomedex.com

This is an amazing conference that focuses more heavily on trends and technology but it is perfect if you like to learn about new things. Takes place in August in Seattle, WA.

Can't travel? That's okay.

• MeetUp

http://www.meetup.com

There are tons of bloggers meeting up for drinks in every city and state in the US and abroad, so log in and join a group. I randomly joined the podcasting NYC group and out of it have met some of my closest allies in the business. Highly Recommended and FREE!

WEEK 6: CONNECTING WITH FANS VIA YOUR NEWSLETTER LIST & CONDUCTING SURVEYS

THINKING OF YOURSELF AS A COMMODITY, AND YOUR FAN AS A CUSTOMER

This week's lesson could be the difference between you making a little money off of your music vs. making A LOT of money.

Before we dive in... You may be freaking out here a bit. In your mind your fans are NOT customers. Your fans don't "buy" from you and you do not consider them in that light – and I totally understand this. But, I am asking you to take off your artist hat for a minute and put on your business hat. In order to be successful you must think about your fans as customers.

All of the current news surrounding the music business is bad news. Record industry veterans are getting laid off left and right and CD sales continue to drop as consumers get free music online. The old music business is still stuck in the same old pattern: sell one CD each to a million people (or many millions) and SUCCESS! This strategy is all about selling *limited things:* CDs, downloads, ring tones etc.

It's no longer sufficient to have only CDs and downloadable tracks for sale, because in your customer's mind there is little to no value attached to CDs and downloads – and working to your disadvantage is that free downloads are readily available everywhere online.

This is an exciting time to come up with some alternatives and create some offerings for your core fan base that will, in the long run, make you a lot more money. It's time to break the mold and create something that is more sustainable for you as an artist.

The new paradigm should be a two-pronged approach:

Sell *MANY things* to a smaller group of your core people who know, love and trust you and want to come back to you and to your brand many times for more.

Create a sense of belonging and community around your music. By doing this your fans will feel like they are members of a club and not just buying a one-time thing.

How will you achieve this?

It will take some time and strategy.

1,000 TRUE FANS

Before you read the rest of this chapter I highly recommend you read 1,000 True Fans: http://tinyurl.com/1000TrueFans, it's one of the most important articles written about making money in today's swiftly shifting new music business and it's mentioned by the experts at every key music conference and referenced in almost all forward-thinking conversations about today's new music business.

THE FIRST STEP: BUILD RAPPORT WITH YOUR EMAIL LIST.

This comes down to communicating regularly and consistently with your fan base and then – when the time is right – asking them for money.

I have seen it countless times: artists totally misuse their email lists by ONLY reaching out to their fans when they have something to SELL them (a show, a new release, etc.) but they never reach out to their fans for other reasons (to share news, say hi, ask their opinions, invite them out for a drink, and get them more involved with you).

Many artists I work with argue with me on this point and say that their fans get angry with them if they communicate with their lists too much.

If someone does not want to receive communications from you, that's okay. Remove them from your list. People who ask to be removed from the list probably won't buy from you anyway, so remove them with joy and get on with bonding with the core fan base that really wants to hear from you.

WRITTEN EXERCISE: A BRAINSTORMING EXERCISE – CREATING RAPPORT:

Here are some ideas on how to improve your monthly newsletters. Start to think about ways to get fans to open and read your emails, and why they look forward to receiving them.

Answer The Following Questions:

Who Are Your Fans?

• Are they male or female?

• Singles or couples?

• How old are they?

• How much money do they make on average?

What Do They Like To Do?

• Is there an activity / hobby they like? Skiing? Surfing? Hiking with their dogs? Wine tasting?

• When they are not seeing live music, what do they do? Movies? Restaurants? Parties?

• If you were hanging out with a cross-section of them at a party, what would they be talking about? Their families/kids? Their classes in school? What else?

Where Do They Hang Out?

- Bars

- Restaurants

- Dance clubs

- Yoga class

- Gym

- Skate park

- Mommy groups

- The mall

- Coffee shop

- High School

- College

- Other?

- Do they go on vacation? Is it hot or cold? Are they with family? Do they travel in groups? Etc.

What Websites Do They Congregate On?

- MySpace

- Facebook

- LinkedIn

- Flickr

- Blogs

- Twitter

- Other

Other Questions:

- Do they like blogs or podcasts or other new media outlets?   Or are computers intimidating to them?

- What magazines or books do they read?

- Do they like sports?   Which ones?

- Do they meet or spend time together outside of your shows?

Sum it Up

Now look over your answers, go back and circle the responses that have a consistent theme or a few themes.   Write those observations below:

Choose Some Themes

If they are your fans, then you will share a lot of the same hobbies and traits with them.   What could you add to your monthly / bi-monthly newsletter that would engage them, based on what you have brainstormed?

CREATING AN ENGAGING NEWSLETTER – THE THREE G'S: GREETING, GUTS & GETTING

At the very top of the newsletter, sum up what is about to follow so people know what is coming in your newsletter.

PART 1. GREETING – MAKE IT PERSONAL

An introduction from you and some personal information – share something non-music related here. A wrap-up of what you have been up to such as a vacation, family time, what you are reading, or listening to, TV and movies you are watching and why you liked them, etc. Post photos of these personal touches on Flickr, Facebook, MySpace, your homepage, etc.

PART 2. GUTS - THE MEAT OF YOUR NEWSLETTER

The meat of the newsletter – What you as an artist (or the band) have been up to. Are you in the studio? On the road? Writing new tracks?

Remember people love and connect to stories, so TELL STORIES.

PART 3. GETTING - PUT READERS INTO ACTION

This is the part of the newsletter that gets your fans to take action on your part:

- Ask them to join your network on another site (Facebook, Twitter, Flickr, MySpace, etc.)

- Ask them to vote for you in an online contest

- Ask them to review your CD on CD Baby, iTunes or Amazon

- Give them a survey to fill out or a contest to participate in

- Gift them a free download – a special gift makes you memorable

- Invite them to an upcoming show

- Invite them to buy your music on iTunes or at CD Baby

- Invite them to listen to a new track on MySpace

> **TIP:** There should only be ONE "Get" (call to action) per newsletter. Fans will get confused and overwhelmed if you have more than that.

SURVEYS: HOW TO ASK YOUR FANS WHAT THEY WANT

Before you assume what it is your fans would like from you, I suggest that you conduct a free survey and ask them!

There is a great website called Survey Monkey where you can create a FREE survey of up to 10 questions and send it around to your list for feedback. If you want to do a complete, in-depth survey, it's only $19.99 per month.

http://www.surveymonkey.com

The MOST SUCCESSFUL marketers ALWAYS test the waters before they release anything. A survey can help you create as a brand and launch a product line that caters directly to your fans. After all, it is your fans who will give you money and support your creative work.

There are many things to consider when you look at it in this light:

- What is your product line? Do you only sell CDs? Do you have merch? A fan club? A line of products that you can sell to your fans?

- Do you have a real fan base / email list to sell these things to? I consider a real fan base a MINIMUM of 1,000, but between 5,000-10,000 is a great goal number to work towards.

- Have you ASKED your fans what they are willing to buy, what they want and how much they are willing to spend?

- Have you ever let your fans know they can invite you to play a house or school concert, a backyard party, or a corporate event? You can do this by simply mentioning that you are available for private events in your newsletter.

- Do you have another talent that your fans don't know about? Do you paint? Do you write, etc.?

- Can you create some sort of monthly continuum program that your fans might pay a monthly premium for? How about a live track of the month club or a special new song you are working on? Would your fans pay $2 a month for that? If you think so, that's $24 per fan and that adds up.

SO, TO RECAP:

Build your email list!! Every day think about who you can add to your list. There is a great service called Bandletter that can do it all for you—sign up here:

http://www.bandletter.com

or email Kevin directly (Kevin@Bandletter.com)—tell him I sent you.

When your list gets to be at least 1,000 strong, create a survey that asks them what they would like from you. Create products and fan clubs and house concerts to satisfy your fans and generate more money!

WRITTEN EXERCISE: WRITE DOWN SOME IDEAS FOR YOUR NEXT NEWSLETTER

Go back through this chapter or use the responses from your survey and find some themes and topics that your fans will like. List them here:

1.

2.

3.

4.

5.

6.

You just wrote six—that's 6 months worth of newsletter themes.

NOTES

WEEK 7: HOW TO BUILD YOUR MAILING LIST

THE MOST CRITICAL ASPECT OF YOUR CAREER IN THIS RAPIDLY CHANGING BUSINESS

I believe your email newsletter list is your most valuable asset.

> **Building Your Fan Base = Building Your Email List**
>
> **The Size of Your Email List = The Size of Your Income**

So, how big is yours?

What artists try to tell me is they don't play many (or any) gigs, and therefore they say that there is no need to create a newsletter.

The truth is: most of the artists that I work with don't have *any* shows to promote. If you want to be an artist (whether you play live or not) you still need to get your music and your message out.

To do this, you must communicate something to your fans **regularly** and **consistently.**

If you disappear from the hearts and minds of your fans for several months, they will not know where you've been, and they will disengage. You also want to bear in mind that If you only email your fans when you have a show, or a new CD to sell them, it totally screams, *"Hey fan, I want your money!"*

You just show up out of nowhere and say: *"I know you had no idea where I've been for the last six months, but here, buy something now!"* – and people hate being sold to, and they naturally resist it. People do, however, love to belong and to participate actively in communities, so if you can make them feel like they belong you will be well on your way.

SIX TIPS FOR GETTING MORE FANS ONTO YOUR NEWSLETTER LIST

1. ADD FRIENDS & FAMILY

Mine through your inbox and outbox. We all have them. Huge inboxes stuffed with email from people who you're communicating with. Are they already on your email list? If not, email each of them and ask: "Is it okay for me to add you to my newsletter list?" Be sure to offer a free MP3 and if they say yes, add them!

> **TIP:** Never ever add someone without getting permission first, even if it's a friend, because that's considered SPAM.

Send a simple email that says something like this:

Dear *(NAME)*

I was just mining through my in-box and I came across our last email.

(Say something personal that connects you to this person here – how you met, who you know in common, the last event you attended etc.)

Would it be okay if I add you to my monthly / bimonthly email list? I would love to keep you in the loop about what I am up to as an artist and from time to time I give away free music too!

Please let me know if it's okay with you.

I will never give your email address to anyone else and you can opt out of my list at any time.

Thanks,

Signature File

2. CREATE A SEPARATE IN-BOX FOR POTENTIAL EMAIL SIGN-UPS

Name it –"Potential Newsletter Reader" – and throughout the week when you get an email from someone who you think would make a nice addition to the list, simply move it into that specific box. Then, when it's time for your scheduled hour, sit down and build your list.

3. BRIBE THEM ONTO YOUR LIST – GIVE AWAY A FREE EXCLUSIVE MP3 OR VIDEO

Let's face it—People are motivated by self-interest. Remember, when they come onto your website they are asking the "What's In It For Me?" question in their heads.

Give them a bribe of a free track to incentivise them! Add a box to your homepage that says "sign up to my monthly newsletter and receive an exclusive track from my newest album (or an exclusive live track or video)."

> **TIP:** Do not have this same track available on your MySpace page—make it exclusive to your site only—but DO advertise it there!

4. LIST TRADE WITH ANOTHER BAND

Once you have a sizeable email list, you can approach other bands that you play with or whose music is similar to yours (or maybe they're from your hometown or share some other common interest), and you can ask them to write an endorsement email saying:

"Hey, if you like us, you'll like our friends!"

Then they can send that endorsement out with a request for joining your email list and you can, in turn, do the same for them. Always have a free MP3 as an incentive.

When you do a list trade with another band, always make sure that your music is very well described in a couple of sentences – what you sound like, who you get compared to – so your potential fans will know what to expect.

If you can, take them directly to a page where they can get a free MP3 that's streaming the moment they sign up so they can check you out.

5. GET MOBILE - START A TEXT MESSAGE LIST

Sending a text message to your fans is original and stands out (emails tend not to stand out).

I recommend using a free service to capture mobile/cellular phone numbers called Broadtexter. It's free and you can add their widget to your homepage, MySpace, Facebook etc.

http://www.broadtexter.com

http://www.mozes.com

GigTIP: Before you start playing a gig, when you ask fans to switch off their cell phones, ask them first to text you their information. Then you build a cell phone directory list and you can SMS people directly to their cell phones the next time you're coming through town. This is a totally unique and original way of communicating on people's cellular phones and will get you noticed.

Amanda Palmer did this and got hundreds of new fans on to her list each night by giving out her tour manager's cell phone number. His cell phone was used as a list builder.

6. SCHEDULE A SET TIME EACH WEEK FOR LIST GROWING

Create a time at least once a week to sit down and actively add to your email list. You will be amazed at how many people you meet and come into contact with who you do not add to your list because it slipped your mind, but with some focus you can become a list-building animal.

When I started regularly communicating with the fans on my fan list at Ariel Publicity, magic started happening. My articles started getting picked up and reprinted online. People started leaving me nice messages and saying, "Thank you for your newsletter, your advice made an impact."

I even hosted my first all-day workshop that came directly from people on my newsletter list and it SOLD OUT so fast I had to add a second session!!

Why?

Because I sent emails regularly and consistently, and people began to trust me and like what I had to say – and then I asked them for money.

In other words, I made money by just communicating and asking.

Studies prove that people buy from people they like and trust, and there is no better way to earning people's trust than by communicating with them on a regular basis – something personal and fun or unique about yourself offstage that your fans may not know. So, go out there and build your email list.

LIVE SHOW BONUS: DO A GIVEAWAY / RAFFLE AT EVERY SHOW

When you are playing a show, hold up a CD or a T-shirt on stage and announce you are doing a free give-away and a raffle. Have a friend sweep through the venue with a hat and have everyone drop their business cards into the hat. When the hat reaches the stage, pull a random business card out and do a give-away. If your fans don't have business cards, use note cards they can write on, or use a clipboard.

Have the winner come up to the stage and hold up the CD to show the audience (this is giving yourself and your product a plug in front of everyone and is great subliminal marketing).

Then, mention to the crowd that you're going to add everyone in the hat to your email list. You've just collected a ton of new email names and addresses that you definitely would not have captured.

So to summarize…

Your Main Goal is: GROW YOUR LIST

EXERCISE: SEVEN STEPS TO JUMP-START YOUR MAILING LIST BUILDING RIGHT NOW!

1. Make dates with yourself: Look at your calendar for the next month (and, if you can, for the next 3–6 months) and schedule some time, at least 60–90 minutes, where you will sit down and focus only on building your email list.

2. Create a list of bands / artists who you play with, or are friendly with, who could do a list-trade or an endorsement with you.

3. Draft a "form email" that you keep in a folder on your computer that you can send around to potential list candidates to get their permission (there is one on page 92—simply use it as a backbone and modify it to suit your needs).

4. Go to http://www.broadtexter.com and read through the site – decide if adding a mobile fan list is the right choice for you and if you want to add this widget to your homepage and your social networking sites asap.

5. Contact your web designer and have him add a "bribe" or a free and exclusive downloadable MP3 to your homepage immediately so that you can capture more people who visit your site.

6. Go to http://www.tinyurl.com/reverbfreebribe and grab the "Exclusive Downloads" widget (there are many other wonderful widgets available here as well). Add these widgets to your MySpace page and to Facebook (and all social Media sites) to capture more signups.

7. Go through all of your MySpace friends and send an individual email to each one asking them if they would like to join your email list by asking them for their email addresses.

> **TIP:** The best way to get someone to give you his email address from MySpace is to compliment him on his MySpace page (music, etc.) and be authentic.

NOTES

WEEK 8: REAL LIVE NETWORKING TIPS

HOW TO GET PEOPLE ON YOUR MAILING LIST IN PERSON

A major lesson you have been getting out of this program so far is the importance of getting people on your email list.

Here are some real life *Networking 101* tips that I learned from sales and networking guru Larry Sharpe. Larry is such a master at networking that people literally line up to talk to him at parties and events.

There Are Three Reasons Why We Network:

1. To find a direct target or customer. For example, a fan that will buy tickets, music, or merch and support you (but first you need to get them on your email list and build rapport).

2. To gain a sphere of influence, and therefore a source for referrals (i.e. people who like the people that know and support your music/brand/band).

3. As a resource for you and your customers (I'm calling fans "customers").

When You Go into Any Networking / Social Situation:

The biggest goal of networking is: Be memorable.

How do you do that?

Simple: The more that *they* talk, the more memorable *you* are.

ON FIRST CONTACT

When you meet people, first ask a question about THEM: "What brought you here today? How did you meet the bride?" Get them talking.

Never walk up to someone and say: "Hi, I'm David." That makes it all about YOU. Instead, you want to say something like, "So, Nancy, what do you do?" Or, "Are you having a good time?" Or, "What brings you here today?" Then, it's all about THEM.

BUSINESS CARDS

If you don't have one and are above the age of 18, GET A BUSINESS CARD NOW! You have no excuse – they are free. Go here:

http://www.VistaPrint.com

Or design your own and print them:

http://www.jakprints.com

> **TIP:** Put one sentence about your music (your PITCH), and the instrument you play on your card. A card with just a name and an address is totally unmemorable!

> **TIP:** Put a photo of yourself or your band logo on the card to add even more branding and recognition. Make sure you list your email, website and links. I love Moo Cards— http://tinyurl.com/MiniMooCards

Don't worry about giving out your card. Focus on getting *their* cards.

Never give your card out unless someone asks for it. If you give a card, you are selling (people hate selling). If someone asks for your card, they are buying (people love buying).

WHAT NEXT?

After getting people to talk about themselves a little bit and maybe exchanging business cards, follow these ABCs when you go to a party, wedding, or any social situation:

A. Know What to Ask For

For example:

A private gig

A student to teach lessons to

A place to rehearse

…and of course, you can always ask for an email address if you do not have any other specific goal that day.

B. Be a Gatherer

This means that whenever you are in any social situation, you should be gathering as much information as possible about each person: interesting tidbits about them, what they like, who they know, where they go, etc.

> **TIP:** For this, don't think about yourself! Think: *How can I be helpful to this person that I'm talking to?* So, let go of your story and your pitch and let them talk all about themselves.

C. Follow Up

After you get home and it's time to follow up, never send your marketing pitch or talk about your business in the initial email. Get people to respond to your follow-up.

Say something very simple without a pitch, like:

"Dear Leslie, It was nice to meet you. Weren't those little pigs in blankets delicious?"

Then close the email with your name and sig file that has your links to your site, Facebook, Twitter, etc. (for an example see mine on page 76).

If they respond, then you can pitch them. So, remember, the first follow-up is always friendly and positive, and *not* business-oriented!

BE A SHARK IN A SEA OF TUNA

When networking, don't think about your industry. If you are trying to grow your business (and you should always be trying to grow your business), it's helpful to go to the places that are the exact opposite of your industry.

So, as a musician, you would go and network with a bunch of other musicians if you were looking for more people to play with or to tap into a community of musicians. However, this is probably not going to make you money.

If you go to, say, a bridal convention, and you meet a whole bunch of people who are planning weddings, and you introduce yourself as a musician, you might get some really good gigs.

INITIAL FOLLOW-UP ON THE PHONE

Something like, *"Hey, Larry. Laura asked me to give you a call. This is Ariel."* Use only your first name. Never say, *"Hi, my name is Ariel,"* because then people will think of you as a stranger (you would never call your mom and say: *"Hi, my name is Ariel."* It's too formal).

So, just say: *"I'm Ariel,"* or *"This is Ariel,"* and then carry on with your conversation.

Words Never To Say

Words that you should never, ever say are:

"I'm just..."

"I'm not looking to sell you anything..."

"I'm not looking for connections..."

Don't use these to try to put them at ease because the person will immediately think the opposite. The brain doesn't register "I'm just..."

WHEN IT'S YOUR TURN TO TALK: HOW TO POSITION YOURSELF

When they are finally engaged with you (after they have talked about themselves) and you are ready to make your pitch, talk about what other people say about you, instead of pitching yourself.

Why? Because people always believe what other people say about you more than they believe you saying it about yourself!

So, you could say something like: "People say my music sounds like Bob Dylan crossed with a touch of The Beatles." Or, "My voice gets compared to Annie Lennox."

This will register very well.

EXERCISE: MENTALLY PREPARING FOR WHAT YOU WANT BEFORE YOU GO OUT

Okay, you are ready to go to a party, a wedding, an event for a friend... whatever.

This exercise takes 5 minutes....

• Go to a quiet place

• Take a deep breath

• Focus on what it is you would like today, this week, this month, to move your musical career forward

• If you need to, write down the one or two things you would like

• The default thing you can always ask for is a business card so you can grow your email list

• Keep that thing in mind when you walk out of the door

Really want it?

Before you walk in the room, touch your head and repeat to yourself the exact thing/things that you want.

Now follow all of the tips above.

WEEK 9: CREATING A CONTINUUM PROGRAM

GETTING YOUR FANS TO BUY FROM YOU OVER AND OVER AGAIN

I have spent the last few years taking many Internet marketing courses and attending seminars. Some were centered on overall Internet marketing, like *Armand Morin's Big Seminar,* and some were hyper-focused on niche markets, like *Podcamp* (podcasting) and *Gnomedex* (blogging). I have also listened to many wonderful audio programs and I am a business book junkie.

This week's module deals with Continuum Programs, which are the number-one way that Internet marketers (also called infoprenuers) make boatloads of money.

So, Before We Move Ahead I Want To Recap What You Have Already Accomplished And Implemented:

• Your newsletter is going out at least once or twice a month

• Your email list is steadily growing

• You are taking the time out to build your list at least once a week for an hour

• You have surveyed your core fans and you know what it is that they want

Now, it's time to start thinking about creating and rolling out your Continuum Program. This is an offer to get your fans to buy from you on a regular basis.

The concept is simple: Get your fans to give you money on a consistent basis – but you can only do this after they have come to trust you and they have proven that they want to buy from you.

Remember the Columbia Records program? Their concept was simple: give the music-lover customer a LOT of value (12 cassettes for $1) – then offer them albums they will like, based on their tastes, for a monthly premium.

So, what can you offer your fans on an ongoing basis that will get them to buy?

Note this does not have to be an every-single-month buy: It can be four times a year – the concept here is consistency! And it's a great idea to think in a "funnel-like" manner so that as you add new people to your list and fanbase they can opt in at anytime.

THE FUNNEL – A BASIC MARKETING PRINCIPLE THAT MAKES YOU MONEY

The marketing funnel is the way that smart businesses make money – a lot of money. The principle is simple to grasp and makes sense to musicians because so many musicians are already doing the top few layers of the funnel.

At the very opening (to get fans into the funnel) you make a free offer that they can't refuse, in exchange for their email address. An exclusive MP3 or a video are both really effective freebies.

Once the fan is in the funnel, and you are sending them regular communications, you can ask them to pay for something – like a download for 99 cents, or a ticket to a show, or perhaps a full album.

The idea of the funnel is the more loyal, engaged, and interested your fan becomes, the more money he will be willing to spend on you, as he or she moves down the funnel.

As the funnel gets smaller you want to add more expensive items to it.

The idea is that the most diehard and engaged fans who love you the most will buy many things from you, and hopefully everything you have to offer!

Here is what a funnel looks like:

FREE MP3 or Video (exclusively on your site in exchange for their email address)

99 Cent Download

$8 - $15 Full Album / Concert Ticket

$2 a Month Club - 1 Song Per Month or Week

$20 - $25 - T-Shirt, Hat, Cooler, Cool Merch

$47 - Special Event

$250 - $500 Private Show

$1000 Custom Written Song - Personalised

EXERCISE: CREATING YOUR FUNNEL

Here is a blank funnel for you to fill in. (Actually I provided three blank funnels, because over the course of the next few weeks or months they may change as you create new ideas and products to sell).

Fill One In:

Don't worry if you don't already have some of the things you will be adding to the funnel – JUST WRITE!

Date:

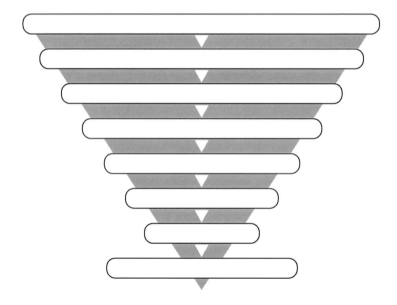

Date:

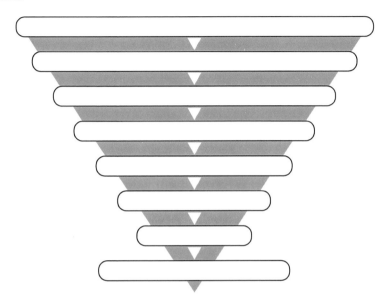

Date:

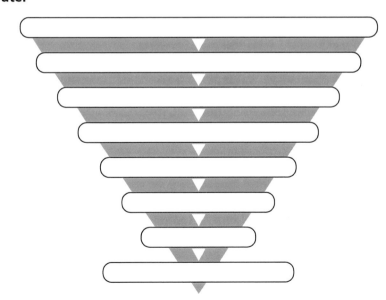

Here are some ideas for a range of expensive things for your funnel:

CONTINUUM PROGRAM IDEAS:

1. Monthly Fan Club

Record a unique track or video once a month and charge your fans a small fee to join the club ($2 -$3 a month).

2. Special Events With The Band Club

Create a fan club that hosts four to six special events a year. Not all of them have to be you performing. You can get creative. Have a wine tasting or a dessert party or a pub crawl. Get local businesses involved by holding these events on a slow night, like a Monday, or during a down month for the business (January can be slow for a lot of restaurants).

3. Artist Critique and Feedback

Invite your biggest fans to come hear the songs that you've written for a new album. Play them in an acoustic setting around a big circle. Give them cards and let them vote on the songs they like. This makes your fans feel extra included because they can help you choose what will make it onto you new record.

4. Private Gigs

You can play a dinner party or a backyard BBQ, or a coffee shop gig that's private-invite only. You could arrange these two to four times per year. Announce the fact that you are available to play private gigs in your bi-monthly newsletter.

5. Monthly Gifts

Do a special promotion each month. Can you think of any ideas that would work as part of a Continuum Program?

6. An Event for Each Season

How about a concert for each season? This would be a great way to get fans to pay four times a year. Hold a quarterly concert with a theme, such as Halloween, Valentine's Day, Summer Solstice, April Fools, or Winter Wonderland.

7. Annual Camping Festival

I worked with a band called **ekoostik hookah** for many years, and they held a camping festival twice a year in their home state of Ohio. These festivals attracted thousands of fans from across the whole state, who paid big bucks to spend Labor Day and Memorial Day with the band and see them play with other artists. **moe** also does this with their annual **moedown** festival. These events made them tens of thousands of dollars.

8. Be the Belle of the Ball

There's a band in New York City called **Valeze** that built a cult following by decorating the venues each time they played with streamers and balloons. They would have a theme like "circus" or "disco," and everybody would get decked out and attend the shows, which became great parties because they were truly special events.

9. Charity Affiliation

Affiliate with a charity and donate a portion of your monthly or event proceeds to that chosen charity. Then your fans will be keeping you, their favorite artist, in business while supporting a charity at the same time, which will make them feel like they are giving back. Align with a local charity in your hometown and get them to support you as well.

10. Private VIP Fan Website

Create a special website that only your fans can access. On it, offer them special things like wallpapers, screen savers, and other bonus gifts. You could also create a special paid podcast, once per month, where you not only play your own music but also recommend other artists that they might like, or interview your favorite artists.

11. Item Of The Month Club

It could be a ski hat in February and a tank top in August. Could you create a fun item of the month club for fans?

How much could you charge for any or all of these ideas?

Do The Math!

If you charge just 200 fans $5 per month to be in your top-tier fan club with exclusive offers and membership just for them, that equals $12,000 a year in extra income. And you can set it up so that PayPal puts that money directly into your bank account on a monthly basis.

If you charge 1,000 fans $2 a month to be in your song of the week / month club, that's $24,000 a year!

EXERCISE: CONTINUUM PROGRAM IDEA GENERATION

Go over the 10 ideas that I outlined above and circle one or two that could work for you and your music and fans.

Write down one idea that caters to your fans that you could introduce within the next 3 months as an added way to produce income:

WRITTEN EXERCISE: COMPLETING YOUR FUNNEL

Now write down the things you will need to do in order to get the funnel complete.

For example:

- Order t-shirts

- Record a song a week / month

- Create extra video content for free offer

- Research where to have a dinner party / costume ball

- Select a charity that you feel is right for you to align with

6 IDEAS FOR GETTING YOUR FUNNEL FILLED IN

1.

2.

3.

4.

5.

6.

BONUS CHAPTER: TRADITIONAL PR PART 1 – AN OVERVIEW

- ## EIGHT SIMPLE STEPS TO FORMATTING A PROPER PRESS RELEASE

- ## HOW TO BE YOUR OWN PUBLICIST: A STEP-BY-STEP GUIDE TO GARNERING MAXIMUM ATTENTION

- ## HOW TO POST A PERFECT PRESS KIT ON YOUR WEBSITE

I believe it is critical to understand the basics of publicity in order to advance your career. In this section, I will go over how to write a standard press release – which you may need to do from time to time when you need to approach the traditional media – and provide a full overview of traditional PR and how to do it. You may never want to or have to, but I think it's important to understand the full scope of how PR works so if you ever hire or manage a publicist you will understand the structure and oversee their work to make sure that they are serving you well.

I often go on and on about how I personally abandoned "traditional" PR, but it still has its place, and it can produce fruitful results when handled properly. I encourage all artists to include it as part of their outreach strategy.

EIGHT SIMPLE STEPS TO FORMATTING A PROPER PRESS RELEASE

A press release should be one page only and on letterhead (I know fewer and fewer people actually have official letterhead) – what I mean is, put your logo or your record company's logo at the top.

Your press release should be formatted like this:

1. TOP LINE: "FOR IMMEDIATE RELEASE"

All press releases start with **FOR IMMEDIATE RELEASE-** written in the top left hand corner, and always in CAPS and underlined.

2. THE CONTACT INFORMATION

Contact Info should include your first and last name (or the first and last name of your contact person), a phone number and an email address. The web address is optional here, or you can include it at the bottom in the additional contact information section.

The top of the Press Release should look like this:

FOR IMMEDIATE RELEASE

Contact: Ariel Hyatt (212) 239-8384 Contact@ArielPublicity.com

3. HEADLINE

Next comes the headline of the press release, which should be simple, centered and bold. An example:

Jen Chapin to Celebrate Release of New Album with East Coast Tour

4. SUBHEAD

This is an expanded part of the headline, which brings the reader in and accentuates the headline by adding detail.

An example:

The daughter of the late great Harry Chapin is heading out on a 10-city tour to support Ready, her new album on Metropolitan Hybrid.

Tour stops will Include Philadelphia, Boston, Portland, and Hartford.

5. OPENING PARAGRAPH: LOCATION, DATE & 5W'S

The opening paragraph should start with *(City, State) Date* – This is so the reader knows where the information is coming from and how timely the information is.

Example: **(New York, NY) June 20, 2010**

And it should answer the 5W's: *Who, What, When, Where and Why.*

This initial paragraph should always grab the reader and answer all of the basic questions the reader might have. These are factual. If the release is to promote a show or a specific event, include the full date, venue name, venue address, show time, ticket price and ages as well as a link to the venue for further directions and information.

6. SECOND PARAGRAPH: USP / UNIQUE SELLING POINT AND QUOTES

This is the "meat" of your press release, so make it juicy!

This will include further information, more details, an engaging story, a quote about your music or about the topic of the release from reviewers, fans, a producer, a venue owner or an industry tastemaker (because what other people say is always taken more seriously and is more believable than your own hype). Your PITCH from Chapter 2 should also be included here (pretend that the reader may never actually hear the CD).

7. FINAL DETAILS & ADDITIONAL CONTACT INFORMATION

Here is where you would include all tour dates, a mailing address, a link to your websites, and a place where a photo can be downloaded. A link where the CD or tracks can be purchased and a label contact can also be added here.

8. THE 3 # # #'S -THE END!

Now type this: ###

This indicates that the press release is finished and there is not another page.

HOW TO BE YOUR OWN PUBLICIST: A STEP-BY-STEP GUIDE TO GARNERING MAXIMUM ATTENTION

I wrote a little article back in the late '90s that was re-published in many places including *The Indie Bible*, at *Colorado Music.Org,* in *Womanrock* and in print at *Nightflying,* and since then many artists have come up to me at conferences, called and emailed to say thanks for writing that article –"I followed what you said and I got results!" It's been updated every year since and here it is….

INTRO –THE STATE OF MUSIC PUBLICITY NOW

Music publicity has changed radically in the past few years. Gone are the days when just having a CD was considered a shoe-in, and gone, too, are the days where staying on the road for 6-10 months a year guaranteed a good living.

Here are the days of *ProTools,* cheap CD manufacturing (or DIY at home with a color printer) and the Internet… immediate access to free music and total information overload at the tip of your fingers!

There are more bands on the road than ever before, over 1,000 brand-new releases each and every week – and fewer and fewer traditional media outlets writing about independent new music. This combination, from a traditional publicist's perspective, is lethal. However, it is still possible for an indie artist to get attention.

Publicity, like building a fanbase, takes time, dedication and effort. When you are doing a PR campaign the effort is sometimes Herculean compared to the result (if you gauge the result solely on how many articles get written).

Publicity is time-consuming and detail-oriented. But with a bit of planning and focus, you can spin your own publicity wheel – all it takes is foresight, organization and patience.

The artist who plans well and understands publicity is the artist who receives the most PR. The good news is that the publicity process for any band, no matter how big or small, is very much the same. Of course, the size of the publications in which you place articles can vary dramatically (this is based on what style of music is hot at the moment, combined with record sales and label status).

For this article, I interviewed two music journalists. Their comments and advice are included throughout. I also included several web links to help you along. The two writers I have quoted here are:

Kristi Singer – Writes for: *American Songwriter, Singer & Musician Magazine, Sun News* and *The Wilmington Star News,* among others.

Waleed Rashidi – Writes for: *Alternative Press, Modern Drummer, Alarm, MeanStreet, Law of Inertia,* and *e-online,* among others.

It was fun to interview writers who usually interview my artists. It provided a lot of insight to get their opinions on what they like to see from bands – as well as what they don't.

PART ONE –THE PRINTED PRESS KIT

A printed press kit is a critical component to add when sending out your CD to anyone in the industry who needs to understand the details and background information on you. Your press kit that goes out to journalists should vary slightly from the one you send out to get gigs (this one should include all four elements listed on the next page PLUS past touring history in detail, as well as your stage plot).

MYTH: I don't need a press kit – people can see all of my information on my website.

TRUTH: Your press kit is still a vital and important component to your overall marketing strategy.

Writers are very busy people who are constantly under deadline, so don't EVER make a writer work to get information about your band. Press kits help them access information quickly and efficiently. A big fat press kit in a folder won't impress. Writers will only become exasperated by a press kit that is not succinct and to the point.

THE 4 STEPS:

The first step in your journey is to create a press kit, which consists of four steps:

1. The bio

2. The photo postcard

3. Articles, quotes and CD reviews

4. The CD

STEP 1: The Bio

Create a one-page bio that is succinct and interesting to read. I strongly advise hiring a bio writer if you can afford one.

If you are not ready to pony up the cash, enlist an outside source to help you out. I find that people who are great storytellers make great bio writers.

> **TIP:** Many music journalists write bios as well as articles, so if you read a great profile on a band in a local paper, on a blog, in an online 'zine, or in a music magazine, don't hesitate – track that writer down and ask him if he or she writes band or artist bios. I suggest updating your bio yourself every few months to keep it fresh and current.

Waleed: "A bio does not have to be extensive. I want a general idea of the band's history and some key shows (but please, not a whole show history). I love the "recommended if you like" line. I know some artists hate to compare themselves to others but I definitely like that – it makes the sorting process easier."

Include your Pitch / USP (Unique Selling Point) towards the top of the page. Create an introduction that sums up your sound, style and attitude in a few brief sentences. This way, if a writer is pressed for time, he can simply take a sentence or two from your bio and place it directly in the publication. If you try to make a writer dig deeply for the gist, that writer will most likely put your press kit aside and look to one of the other 30 press kits that arrived that week.

Avoid vague clichés such as: melodic, brilliant harmonies, masterful guitar playing, tight rhythm section, etc. These are terms that can be used to describe any artist and music.

> **TIP:** Try to create a bio with the assumption that the vast majority of music writers may never get around to listening to your CD. Also, writers are usually under tight deadlines to produce copy, so many CDs fall by the wayside. But that doesn't mean that you can't get a great calendar pick or photo inclusion.

STEP 2: The Photo

It is very tough to create a great band photo. In the thousands I have encountered, only a few have had creativity and depth. It is vital to arrange a photo shoot, and take this seriously. You will benefit from it in the long run.

Create a photo that is clear, light, and attention-grabbing. Five musicians sitting on a couch or backed against a brick wall is not interesting. If you have a friend who knows how to use PhotoShop, I recommend you enroll him or her to help you do some funky editing.

MYTH: We need to have 8″ x 10″ photos.

TRUTH: Gone are the days of the 8″ x 10″. Color postcards are more versatile, and newspapers will download the photos they will run directly from your website.

While 8″ x10″ Photos used to be the industry standard, they are no longer the norm. My company recommends printing 3″ x 5″ or 4″ x 6″ double-sided 4-color postcards. They look great and very professional – and any extra postcards that are not used in press kits can be sent to people on your mailing list, or you can give them away at gigs.

You must make sure your photo is easily downloadable in hi res (300 dpi) on your website so journalists who want images can get them easily. Make sure that the jpg appears PROPERLY LABELED after it is downloaded, with your name and the names of band members from left to right.

I suggest putting several color images, both vertical and horizontal, on your photos page, so editors can choose the ones they like best and which work for their layout. Include your album cover for download as well, so if they run a CD review they can have album artwork with it.

Postcards should have an image of the band on one side and an image of your album cover with the URL of your website on the other side. You can also include your release date of an upcoming album, your contact numbers and a quote about the band's sound from the media or from your bio.

There are many great inexpensive printers available online. We order our postcards from:

http://www.jakprints.com

or

http://www.1800postcards.com

Waleed: "The best types of photos are ones that are crop-able in a vertical or horizontal format; sometimes when I have to fill a hole in the magazine I may need a photo that will fit it into any frame. I also like photos that have room around the photo – this way I can put text around the photo. I want a photo that depicts a band in the way they are. A junkie band should be in a junkyard, a clean band should be in a cleaner atmosphere – environment, wardrobe and location are all very important, as is creativity. I get overkill of fisheye lenses and overkill on oversaturated colors; try not to copy too much of what is going on."

TIP: Don't make journalists hunt around for the photos – they will go to someone else's site to grab them. Downloadable color photos should be readily available on your website, and should be at least 300 dpi and easily findable and downloadable with less than 3 clicks.

Put the band members' names from left to right (l-r) under the band photo to give journalists a point of reference. (Many publications publish photos with all band members' names from left to right to save the writers the trouble of having to ask for the names.)

STEP 3: The Articles, Quotes and CD Reviews

Getting that first article written about you can feel daunting. Two great places to start are your local hometown papers (assuming that you don't live in NYC or Los Angeles) and any music website that you like.

TIP: You can archive additional articles on your website, and if a writer wants to read more than that, he can visit your site for further information. If you don't have anything written about you yet, not to worry – this will soon change.

> **TIP:** Use Google, Twitter, MySpace, and Facebook as resources. to find reviewers you want to contact, or work backwards and search for indie bands that you would be compared to.

Call or email the reviewers that wrote about them, politely introduce yourself and ask if you can send them your CD for consideration. This is a much better technique than the old-school method of getting a "media list" and blindly mailing precious materials out in bulk.

Always Follow Up

Kristi: "Seventy-five percent of all bands don't follow up with me aggressively enough – I often am on deadline and I will ask a band to call me back in a week and most never do."

I keep new CDs in 3 piles in my office:

1. The one I am about to write about because it is assigned.

2. The one I really want to pitch to my editors because I think they will like it.

3. The CDs that I have no idea what they are, and no one followed up with me on them, so I never get to them.

There could be some wonderful and appropriate CDs sitting in my office that I could write about, but if no one pitched me on them they usually get overlooked.

Waleed: "I think it is important to follow up on all mailings. Seventy-five to eighty percent of indie bands that send me stuff never follow up, and those CDs always fall through the cracks."

STEP 4: The CD

The CD artwork, like the press kit, must be well thought out. You should customize your press kits so that they look in sync with your CD. This way, when a writer opens up a package the press kit and the CD look like they go together. Do not bother sending out advance burns of your CD unless the writer requests them. Full artwork is always preferred.

> *Kristi:* "I enjoy getting full artwork CDs – advances and burned CDs are not as intriguing. Presentation is very important."

> *Waleed:* "My micro pet peeve is that I do not like CDs that do not have jewel cases (or at least spines). If a CD is in a baggie or a thin sleeve it makes the CD impossible to find."

A few months ago the "PR List" (a group of music publicists – over 600 of us) ran a survey of music journalists asking them if they would take downloads over CDs. The overwhelming response was: ***Send me the full CD with artwork or don't send anything at all.***

So – for journalists, send the full CD with color artwork and most importantly a READABLE SPINE, so your CD can be found amongst the piles when you call to follow up.

TIP: Put your phone number and contact info in the CD, so if it gets separated from the press kit, the writer knows how to contact you. Also, "Recommended Tracks" stickers are great for the press (suggesting no more than two or three selections).

TIP: Don't waste precious CDs. That means only send a CD if you are sure a writer actually writes CD reviews (few newspaper writers are given the space to run them these days, so check first).

Waleed: "I like well-organized packages as well that are stapled together, so I can take a minute to get through it and flip through cohesive info. And PLEASE put contact info EVERYWHERE – on the CD, on the bio and on the photo. We get a lot of glossies with no band name on them, and we sometimes stack photos separately for our photo editors. If there is no name or number or URL on the photos they will never get used."

PART 2 – GETTING THE WORD OUT

INTERNET – GETTING YOUR ONLINE PRESS MATERIALS TOGETHER

First, duplicate your finished press kit electronically. Either make a PDF of it that you can send to writers as attachments or open an account with SonicBids and drop all of your information into an EPK.

http://www.sonicbids.com

YOUR WEBSITE

If you don't already have an updated website that you are proud to show off to the world, get one ASAP! Register a memorable name and remember: .com is much easier than .net or .org

TOUR PRESS – GETTING YOUR PRESS MATERIALS OUT

Start planning PR for any tour six to eight weeks before you hit the road. As soon as a gig is booked, ask the promoter for the club's press list (most clubs have one). Promoters are dependent on this local press to help sell tickets.

Have the press list emailed to you and reach out to the appropriate journalists on it. Don't be shy – you are working with the promoter to make the show happen, and promoters love it when the show is well publicized.

TIP: Ask the promoter which writers like to receive CDs for review and which ones don't need them. Also be sure to ask the promoter who his favorite writers are and which ones will like your style of music.

Kristi: "I really enjoy it when the band adds a personal note with their press kit. A short and sweet note is that extra personal touch that really makes a huge difference."

TIP: If the local promoter has a publicist, let that publicist do her (or his) job. Pack up everything and mail it to the promoter's publicist. This publicist knows the writers in his or her hometown and will be instrumental in helping you.

Don't get territorial about your PR! You should allow anyone who is willing to help to do so.

LOCATING PUBLICATIONS

If the club does not have a press list, you can easily search Google for a good target list.

TIP: With monthly publications, if you are not at least six to eight weeks out, don't bother sending to them.

WORK YOUR NICHE ANGLES

Work any angles you may have – Is the lead singer in the band Jewish or Irish? Is someone in the band a parent? Most major markets have a Jewish publication, an Irish publication and a parenting magazine, and these are great angles to work.

> **TIP:** Many smaller local publications only cover events and people from certain areas, so if someone in the band is from the town where you are touring, make sure you let the local editors know.

FOLLOWING UP IS CRITICAL

It is critical that you follow up. As you read in Part 1 of this article, 75% of all indie bands never follow up and writers do not include bands that they don't know if they do not hear from them. When you call the writers, understand that you will be leaving messages 90% of the time.

Leave short and sweet messages that include your phone number and email address as well as your show date and venue to spark the writer's memory. Nine times out of ten, writers will not call you back; that's okay, because you have given them everything they will need.

If you do get them on the phone, don't be afraid to say which promoter recommended you, and always invite them to the show. Don't let all that voicemail discourage you. I have placed hundreds of articles, mentions, and photos without ever speaking to the writer.

> *Waleed:* "The one piece of advice I would give an indie artist is: Be tactful about your pitches and be mindful that writers have to listen to you as well as thousands of other bands in any given month – but also don't be afraid to reach out. It is a journalist's job to listen to new music. Don't give up, but at the same time don't bombard; be mindful not only about your career but also about their careers as well."

PERSEVERE

The first few times you play a market, you may not get any press. If you are a totally new band and you are worried because a paper did not cover you the first time around, keep sending that paper information every time you play in the area. I have never met a writer who ignores several press kits from the same band sent over and over again. It may take a few tours through in each market, but the more a writer sees you over time, the more likely he will be to write about you.

HAVE PATIENCE

PR is a slow-moving vehicle that can take time to get results. I have worked with some bands that needed to go through a market three or four times before any results started showing up in the press.

When you send materials on repeated occasions, include a refresher blurb to remind the writer of your style. Always include the following information: date, show time, ages, ticket price, club name and address, and who is on the bill. Don't make writers hunt around for event info. Make their job as easy as possible by providing all the information.

Also keep in mind that some writers will probably not write about you over and over again. If you hit the same markets continually, a great tactic is to change your postcard every few months.

BONUS ROUND - MORE MARKETING ELEMENTS

POSTERS

Posters are a great form of PR and they don't have to cost you a fortune. I highly recommend 4-color posters, and it's a good idea to create a space on the bottom where you or the promoter can fill in the show info.

The most cost-effective way to make posters is to buy 11" x 17" colored paper from your local paper store (comes in reams of 500) and run off copies at the copy shop (approx. 10 cents each). Make several copies on white paper and include these with your colored posters – this way the promoter can make extras, if needed.

TIP: Make sure you ask the promoters how many posters they would like and send them along with the press kits. After a few days, it's best to call and verify that the posters and press materials were received and are hanging up in the venue.

YOUR STREET TEAM – VIRTUAL OR REAL-WORLD

Enroll your biggest fan to be the head of your street team. Put this person in charge of reaching out to other fans who will join the street team in each market you visit.

In exchange for a few tickets to your show, some merch and some love from you, your field staff will put up posters, hand out fliers and postcards, and talk to their college newspaper about writing a feature or the local radio station about spinning your CD.

If you are not playing out, that's okay – they can help you manage your online portals, and hit all social networking sites to get the word out about you and your music.

TIP: Street Team Management: To get a street team started, include a sign-up column on your mailing list and a form to fill out on your website. Manage your street team using the FREE tools at: http://www.reverbnation.com

WRITTEN EXERCISE: YOUR OWN PRESS KIT ANALYSIS

(Note: If you do not have a press kit yet, you can skip this one!)

Nothing is more effective in making improvements than taking a step back and reassessing. A few times a year you should take yourself through this exercise in order to make your presentation as good as it can be.

Pull out your press kit – either the physical version or the one on your website.

BIO RE-VAMP:

Read over your bio and write down the following things:

Is the overall tone of your bio an interesting and captivating story, or is it a résumé of things that you have done? (If your answer is "résumé," it's time for a re-write!)

Where does your bio first take your reader?

Does the introduction (the first few lines) bring the reader in? Is it interesting or does it use the classic band mistake words such as "unique," "melodic," etc.?

or "the (name of band) started playing music together in 2001"......

BORING!!

Are there other clichés you could avoid, like explaining each song on the album and what it means, etc.? Keep in mind the reader possibly has not listened to any of your music. Circle the clichés or write them here:

Is your pitch located somewhere within the first few lines so people can get an immediate hit of what you are all about? Re-write the beginning of your bio to include a sentence that draws in the reader and contains your pitch so that the reader becomes instantly engaged:

What is the most interesting thing about you / your band as a STORY?

Would this bio be captivating to people who have never met you – if not, is there a missing aspect that you could add to make it more enticing?

Aside from bio editing, what aspects of your overall press kit could you improve?

For example:

Design Layout / Format / Type Style / Graphic Elements / Photos

Stories / Testimonials

Stronger Press Quotes

Niche Angles

– are they all included?

> **TIP:** If you need press quotes, ReviewYou can link you to great bloggers for CD reviews guaranteed in two weeks: http://www.reviewyou.com

WRITTEN EXERCISE: GETTING QUOTES TO ADD TO YOUR PRESS KIT

Here's an exercise to help you identify people who you can ask for some quotes to include in your press kit.

PART 1: FANS

Write down the names of your 5 most enthusiastic fans:

1.

2.

3.

4.

5.

PART 2: THE MUSIC INDUSTRY

Who books you at clubs?

Who produced, mixed or mastered your album?

Do you have any friends in bands a bit further along than you who could give you a quote?

Members of the media or Radio DJs. (Don't worry if they have actually written about you. You don't have to have been covered by someone to get a quote from that writer)

Blogs or Websites or 'Zines that have covered you:

PART 3: HOW TO ASK

This part is easy!

People LOVE to be quoted because it's MORE Publicity for THEM, so just concoct a simple email asking if they wouldn't mind providing a quote.

Here is an example of an email that I use:

Subject Line of Email: **Fishing For Compliments....**

> **Dear Joe,**
>
> **I am updating my website by gathering quotes to add to the testimonials section of my site.**
>
> **I would love a quote from you (which I will of course credit you for with a link back to your website).**
>
> **Might I be so bold as to ask for a quote about your experience working with us (or coming to our shows)?**
>
> **Thanks, Ariel**

HOW TO POST A PERFECT PRESS KIT ON YOUR WEBSITE

I am amazed how hard it can be to find simple press components on many artists' websites.

Here are three critical components that you should include on the press page of your website.

These tips show that you keep music writers and calendar editors in mind. Editors need access to your information quickly, because they are constantly under deadline.

If you do not make it easy for them to get your information from your site, they may move onto another one of the 50 artists that are playing their market that same week.

1. YOUR MUSIC – ALBUM OR LIVE TRACKS

Make sure you have some music available at your website or a very obvious link to your MySpace page where people can hear the music instantly. Many newspapers are now including MP3s of artists coming to town in the online versions of their papers, so make it easy for them to grab the tracks to add to their own sites – this is additional excellent exposure for you.

2. BIOGRAPHY – MUST INCLUDE YOUR PITCH

Make sure you have a short, succinct bio that can be easily located on your site, in addition to the long form one, the blogs and all of the opinions from each band member – which are fun for your fans but not for music writers who will be looking to get quick information. Make sure this bio can be easily cut-and-pasted so writers can drop it into a preview or a column.

USP (Unique Selling Point) – Also include a short summary (less than six words) that sums up your sound for calendar editors.

> **TIP:** MAKE SURE THE BIO CAN BE EASILY CUT-AND-PASTED!

Do NOT have your bio in Flash format; make sure that editors can easily cut and paste it right off of your site.

3. PHOTOS – MAKE THEM EASY TO FIND AND DOWNLOAD

Thumbnails are great for quick and easy loading but are detrimental for use in newspapers. You should always have a few downloadable photos on your site in at least 300 dpi / jpg format.

> **TIP:** Create an easy-to-see link that says "click here for a hi res jpg." That way photo editors can get to them easily. When the photos are downloaded, make sure they are properly named with your name or your band's name, so that photo editors can find them in folders.

> **TIP:** Remember to change your photos a few times a year – so if you play the same markets over and over, you can give the media multiple options for covering you.

> **TIP:** Put the band members' names from left to right (l-r) under the band photo to give journalists a point of reference. (Many publications publish photos with all band members' names from left to right to save the writers the trouble of having to ask for the names.)

4. INCLUDE YOUR ALBUM COVER ARTWORK

You also want to make sure you include your cover art in both hi res and lo res (jpg format). This way if your CD is being reviewed, the writer can download the artwork.

NOTES

BONUS CHAPTER: TRADITIONAL PR PART 2 – A MUSICIAN'S GUIDE TO CHOOSING THE PERFECT PUBLICIST

Here is my guide to choosing a publicist.

I wrote this to help you navigate the ever-expanding world of music PR and offerings in the marketplace, and to help you avoid many of the costly pitfalls my clients have fallen into before they worked with my company. I just got a call last night from a veteran musician who did his homework and avoided hiring one firm with a horrible reputation – only to get all of his money taken by another publicist whose phone was disconnected the day after the check cleared.

I'm not saying this is commonplace in my industry. There are numerous wonderful publicists working hard as you read this, and I have designed this guide as a service to you, so that you can choose the perfect publicist that is just right for you and your team. I totally understand that we were not born with the innate knowledge of what PR is, or how it differs from advertising and other types of promotion you may be looking into – in fact, my first day as an intern at a fancy public relations firm, I asked my supervisor, "What is PR, exactly?" He looked at me like I had ten heads and said, "PR is, well… it's PR!" Hmmm… okay, glad we got that straight, I thought to myself.

Read on to find out more.

SIX MAJOR BENEFITS OF HIRING A GREAT PUBLICIST

There are a lot of good reasons for hiring a wonderful publicist to add to your team.

(I use "she" a lot when referring to publicists because the vast majority are women, no offense to the men in my field.)

1. A publicist can make you look great on paper with a fabulous bio written by a professional. She can also strategize and create a story about you that you may have never thought up.

2. She can help you hone your pitch so you can sell yourself whenever you are talking to anyone.

3. She will increase your name awareness.

4. If you are a touring artist, she can get you tour press in all the local markets where you are scheduled to play.

5. She can get you legitimate press quotes to add to your arsenal, which you can then show your potential team when hiring a radio promoter, retail rep, manager, label, and distribution company. You can also add these quotes to your website and to your press kit.

6. She will save you a ton of work by leveraging her contacts and relationships.

FIVE COMMON MISCONCEPTIONS ABOUT PUBLICISTS & PUBLICITY CAMPAIGNS

Here are some common misconceptions about publicists and publicity campaigns in general.

Misconception Number One: She Sounded Really Together and Ambitious on the Telephone, She Must Be Amazing!

Sometimes yes and sometimes no – a publicist's job is to sell on the telephone and many of them will naturally do a great job of selling themselves to you. Unfortunately, there are a few publicists that have reputations for not delivering great work (or even one single report) after they take your money. So it is critical that you do your research.

Misconception Number Two: By Hiring a Publicist She Can Create Magical Opportunities!

Nope. She can't work miracles, but she can introduce you to the media and help you once you have a defined strategy and a roadmap. Hiring a publicist is just the beginning of your work. You need to keep her busy with stories and angles and events to work throughout her time managing your campaign. A publicist is only as good as whatever she is publicizing, and it is critical to give her as much to use as possible.

Misconception Number Three: She Works For A Huge Band, She Knows All These People, She Will Get Me In *Rolling Stone!*

NO! Publicists should absolutely be hired for who they know, other clients they represent, and their relationships at national publications are critical, but be warned: larger bands, on major labels, with big followings and scaleable sales numbers, get articles over smaller, up-and-coming artists a lot of the time. If you are an emerging artist, you sometimes need to build up to the larger publications.

This does not mean that the publicist should not try to get you placement, she should. Just know that even the tightest personal relationships don't equal articles. Of course, the publicist knows these people and can always ask, but it is absolutely not a guarantee that you're going to get articles written about you.

So you must always strategize about what your angle is before you get into it. And, while national PR is possible for all artists at all levels, it must be appropriately handled. An artist with no national distribution and minimal sales is not likely to end up on the pages of Rolling Stone, Spin, or Blender, unless there is a fabulous story around the band that needs to be told to an international audience.

Misconception Number Four: I'm Gonna Be On National TV!

Television shows such as Late Night, Ellen, and even the Tonight Show do showcase independent artists from time to time – but not all publicists have the connections to get you on these TV shows. In order to avoid a major letdown, discuss this with your publicist before you hire her. You can ask: "Have you ever placed anyone on national TV?" And: "How many artists have played and on which shows?" She will be honest both in her ability to reach the bookers and about what chances she thinks you may have to actually end up on one of these shows.

Misconception Number Five: If I Hire A Publicist, Hundreds Of Articles Will Be Written About Me!

Nope. It is critical to manage your own expectations. I'm not saying aim low, but you must not only have a very compelling story (and of course great music) for anyone to write about you – you must also have a reason to receive media coverage. Just having an album release or a couple of local shows is not actually grounds for national coverage and many larger publications may pass you up the first campaign around. That's okay – this should be considered a building block and not a rejection. Of course playing the numbers does help. So the more appropriate journalists your publicist reaches out to and sends your music to, the better the chances of placements.

NINE CRITICAL THINGS YOU SHOULD KNOW ABOUT PUBLICITY BEFORE YOU MAKE YOUR FIRST MOVE

I talk to musicians all day who call looking to hire a publicist, and I've noticed that many artists don't really understand what publicity is. And why should you? We are not born with this knowledge – and heaven knows I have no idea how to play an instrument.

1. THE DEFINITION OF PUBLICITY

First, we are going to start out with the very basics – some definitions of what publicity is exactly. According to the Merriam-Webster Dictionary:

Publicity – "An act or device designed to attract public interest; specifically: information with news value issued as a means of gaining public attention or support. Also: The dissemination of information or promotional material."

I couldn't have said it better myself. Publicity is EXACTLY these things.

A music publicist is hired as a member of your team to represent you to the media. Media is defined traditionally as editors and writers at newspapers, magazines, college journals, and television. Some publicists may also cover radio for interviews on tour stops, but if you want to get on the radio charts (like CMJ), you will need a radio promoter. Some publicists also cover Internet PR, like my company, but not all traditional publicists do.

A publicist's job is to liaise with the press. They are not hired to get you a booking agent or gig, a label deal, a distribution deal, or any other type of marketing deal. That is what a manager is for. A well-connected publicist may be able to hook you up with all of the above-mentioned things, but it is not in her job description.

2. YOU ARE IN THE DRIVER'S SEAT

Remember, artist – you are the buyer here and you are shopping for PR. You are in the driver's seat. It's your money and your music that keep publicists in business. Hiring a publicist is like hiring another guitar player for your band. Choose one you like, who fits your vision and your goals. All too many times I've heard that a publicist was hired in spite of the artist's personal opinions. You should like your publicist, and she should be the right one for you.

3. WITH PUBLICITY, YOU PAY FOR EFFORT – NEVER FOR RESULTS

I have had disgruntled artists call me and say, "I hired a publicist and I only got six articles. That cost me $1,000 per article!" Sadly, this is not how you quantify a PR campaign. How you quantify a PR campaign is by how many albums were sent out, what the responses were, even if they were inconclusive or negative. You pay for the amount of effort the publicist made on your behalf. Of course, you should get some and even many results. Getting nothing is totally unacceptable. But you never know when your publicist's efforts will show up months, and sometimes years, after your campaign is complete.

4. A PR CAMPAIGN NEEDS TO BE PLANNED WELL IN ADVANCE

For long-lead press (that means magazines with national distribution like *Spin, Rolling Stone* and *Paste*), the editors put their publications to bed three full months before they hit the newsstands. So if your CD is coming out in October, you must have it pressed with full artwork and ready with materials to mail in July. Of course not all PR campaigns focus on national press, but no publicist will take you on with zero lead-time, so you definitely need to prepare lead-time in every case.

Recommended Publicity Campaign Lead Times:

- National Campaign: 3-4 months before the release

- Tour Press Campaign: 4-6 weeks before the show

- Local Campaign: 4-6 weeks before placement

- Online Campaign: 2-3 weeks before placement

(Placement = article, CD review, calendar listing, TV/radio interview, etc.)

5. THE FOUR COMPONENTS OF A PRESS KIT

A good press kit consists of four parts: the bio; the photo; the articles, quotes & CD reviews; and the CD.

The Bio – Create a one-page bio that is succinct and interesting to read. I strongly advise hiring a bio writer (this should cost between $200-$400). If you are not ready to pony up the cash, enlist an outside source to help you. I find people who are great storytellers make great bio writers.

The Photo – Arrange a photo shoot; if you take this seriously, you will benefit deeply. Create a photo that is clear, light, and attention-grabbing. Showing movement is a plus (sitting on a couch or up against a brick wall is not interesting). If you have a friend who knows how to use PhotoShop, enroll him to help you do some funky & fun editing.

The Articles, Quotes & CD Reviews – Getting that first article written about you can feel daunting. Two great places to start are your local hometown papers (assuming you don't live in NYC or Los Angeles), and any music website that you like.

The CD – The CD artwork, like the press kit, must be well thought out. Do not bother sending out advance burns of your CD unless the writer requests them. Full artwork is always preferred. Put your phone number and contact info in the CD so if it gets separated from the press kit, the writer knows how to contact you.

6. PUBLICITY IS A MARATHON, NOT A SPRINT

PR is very different in nature from a radio campaign that has a specific ad date and a chart that you are paying to try to get listed on. There is no top 40 publicity chart. With the sheer number of albums coming out into the marketplace (approx 1,000 per week), it could take months longer than your publicity campaign runs to see results.

7. ONLINE PUBLICITY IS JUST AS IMPORTANT AS OFFLINE PUBLICITY

I would argue that online PR is MORE important, because today's newspaper is tomorrow's recycling. Online publicity goes up fast, and it can be around for months and sometimes for years.

Current research – and sales figures – show that people are reading newspapers less and less with every passing day. More people rely on the Internet as their main news source, and on recommendations from friends, so Internet placements are absolutely wonderful and totally legit.

8. PUBLICITY DOES NOT SELL RECORDS

If you are hiring a publicist to see a spike in your CD sales, I have news for you: There is absolutely no correlation between getting great PR and selling records.

PR is designed to raise awareness of you in the press, to help build a story, and also build up critical acclaim – and, of course, a great article can lead to sales. But overall, if selling albums is your goal, PR is not the only thing you will need to reach it.

9. ALL PUBLICITY IS GOOD PUBLICITY

I know we have all heard this, but it's a great thing to really under-stand. If one of your goals in PR is to get your name out there (and this should be a goal), the truth is that the average person remembers very little of what they read. Only a tiny percentage gets retained, so if you really think that readers are going to remember a tepid or a mediocre review of your CD, the answer is that they won't.

And never ever take your own PR seriously. As my favorite artist Andy Warhol once said, "Don't read your press; weigh it."

MAKING INITIAL CONTACT: THE THREE QUESTIONS TO ASK ANY PUBLICIST FIRST

I get a lot of complaints from artists who call me and say that they tried to get certain PR firms on the telephone, but that they never got a call back or that they had trouble getting them to respond at all. Speaking in defense of a busy PR firm, many of them are just too crazed with work to handle all of the incoming inquiries. However, with a little finesse you can get to them. This is not a guarantee that they will want to take you on as a client, but it will at least get you in the door.

Here is a simple 3-step system that will get you into a conversation with a busy PR firm, after you have done your research and decided which PR firms you would like to target.

But first, a note of precaution & a checklist…

Most major PR firms (the ones that have national acts on their rosters) have strict criteria for accepting clients, and many of them plan campaigns months in advance. So here is a checklist of what you need to have in place before the big firms will be interested:

1. National brick-and-mortar distribution – CD Baby or Tunecore may not be enough of a distribution plan for some larger PR firms who deal with national publications. (Please tell me the last time you read: "Available at CD Baby" in Rolling Stone?)

I'm not saying you need to have national traditional distribution, because personally I don't think it's a great idea for most artists at this point. I'm just letting you know what PR firms sometimes require.

2. A release date that is at LEAST 3-4 months away from your initial contact (preferably 5-6 months).

3. A tour in place or some kind of local or interesting angles to discuss.

STEP 1: PICK UP THE PHONE

Never wimpily email a request to hire a PR firm, it makes you look unprofessional.

When you make initial contact with a public relations firm, don't just dive in and start firing questions at whoever answers the telephone. Note that a very busy intern or an administrative assistant may be in charge of answering the phones and that intern will not be able to tell you prices or PR firm availability, so know who you are talking to and know who to ask for.

> **TIP:** Visit the "about us" section of the PR firm's website and read the names of the people working at the firm, so you know who you may be either speaking to or asking for! And always ask for someone specific by name.

STEP 2: IF YOU ARE ASKED TO LEAVE A MESSAGE, DON'T TAKE IT TO MEAN ANYTHING PERSONALLY

I can't tell you how busy a PR firm with a large roster of clients can be. You will be put into voicemail or someone will take a message. DO NOT just leave your name and phone number!! Leave a full and concise message saying the following:

• Your name – first and last, your band name, and your URL.

- Your telephone number – just ONE number, not work, home and mobile.

- Your reason for calling – "I am interested in hiring a PR firm and I am inquiring about your availability."

If the person asks you for more detail then give it, but don't volunteer your release date and a lot of additional details. That is what the conversation with the appropriate person is for. If no one calls you back within 72 hours, call again and repeat. Three strikes and move on... If a PR firm can't call you back after three tries, then they are not the firm for you.

STEP 2: WHEN YOU GET THE PUBLICIST ON THE PHONE

It is highly probable that the publicist you want to speak to is under deadlines for the day, and you must respect that she has a job to do. So when you do get someone on the phone on first contact, ask only three questions.

But, first introduce yourself very briefly:

"Hi, this is _____ and I'm in a rock band from Los Angeles about to release our new album. "

And here are the three questions:

1. Are you considering new clients for the time frame of _____ (your release date)?

2. Give a very brief synopsis of your project, three sentences max. Include:

   - The genre of music you play

   - Proposed release date

- Distribution plan. It's fine if the album is only digitally distributed or only available through CD Baby, but make sure you tell her that and know this may not be appropriate for her firm

- Your tour schedule with markets and highlights

- Then any other parts of your release plan, like your radio promotion, your retail promotions, your street teams that will be in place, etc.

3. The third question to ask is: *"May I send you my music on CD or links to my MySpace tracks and set up a time to follow up?"*

IS SHE REALLY THAT GOOD? FIVE RESEARCH TIPS TO HELP YOU FIND OUT

Tons of publicists can sound really together and ambitious on the telephone, and they should. This is their JOB. But, sadly, there are quite a few publicists that are known for not delivering great work or being accountable to their clients. So it is critical that you do some due diligence and research.

There are five ways we suggest that you research publicity firms.

1. Google Search the individual names of each publicist, and the name of the company, and look for information about these individuals.

2. Google Search the different bands and artists that the PR firm represents in Google news search and Google blog search, and check out where the placements (articles and stories) have happened. If you don't see a lot of articles on the artists this may not be a great sign.

   http://news.google.com and http://blogs.google.com

3. Check out the CD Baby message boards. There is a lot of information about different publicists on the CD Baby boards,

and clients from these PR firms have talked about their experiences. You can also post and ask for feedback here.

http://cdbaby.org

4. Call the publicists' past clients, management, labels, and artists, and ask them what their experiences were.

5. Sign up for the music thoughts list at

http://groups.yahoo.com/group/musicthoughts

and ask your peers. There are thousands of musicians on this list and they could really help you get some great insights before you spend your money.

HOW TO AVOID FIVE COSTLY PR BILLING RIP OFFS

When you decide to hire a publicist and she quotes you a price, that number usually represents the monthly retainer price. What I want you to be aware of is that on top of that monthly retainer there will be expenses, and you should always ask a simple question to avoid a surprise invoice after your first month onboard with your PR firm.

The simple question is:

"What do you bill for on top of your monthly retainer?"

Here are the 5 common things that a PR firm will bill you for, and some advice on how to save some money. Before we went digital, I created over 1,000 traditional campaigns for artists, and many of them negotiated expenses before the campaign started. It is your right to do so.

#1 – TELEPHONE

A publicist's main tool is the telephone, and the truth is business landlines don't come cheap. A way of avoiding surprises is simply asking *"What is the average monthly charge for the telephone bill?"*

This is usually the same approximate number every month and the publicist will know it and quote you accordingly.

#2 – POSTAGE: REGULAR MAIL, FEDEX, & MESSENGER SERVICES

Mail costs money – this we know, but ask your publicist if she charges a handling fee on top of regular first class postage.

Many do, because they rent postage meters and pay fees for envelope stuffing, plus there is the cost of the labels, meter tape and ink. I know it sounds a little crazy, but until you own a postage meter I can't stress enough that the bloody thing is expensive to maintain!

> **$ Money Saving Tip #1:** Buy stamps, stuff your own envelopes, and send out your own initial mailer. This could save you hundreds of dollars if the PR firm is doing a large mailing on your behalf (over 100 envelopes). Invite your friends, open a bottle of vino and stuff away.

FedEx also costs money, and sometimes a writer is on a deadline and needs a CD the next day, so be prepared.

> **$ Money Saving Tip #2:** Be very aware that your publicist could be using "FedEx First," which costs $5 -$15 more to get it there first thing in the morning. So always have a conversation about what type of FedEx she uses and request "standard delivery" if that is possible.

Messenger services are a necessity and sometimes need to be used. Always ask what the charges are so you are not surprised (it costs approximately $10 to deliver a small envelope in midtown Manhattan).

#3 - COPIES, PAPER & ENVELOPES

If your publicist is putting a press kit together for you, chances are she will be using paper and a copier. Ask how much she charges per page for copies.

> **$ Money Saving Tip #3:** Make the copies yourself at a local copy shop if it costs considerably less than your publicist charges. Drop them by her office by when she needs them, though you must respect her need to do her job with good lead-time.

Padded envelopes are also very costly, so again, if it will save you a good amount of money, buy the envelopes and do the mailer yourself! Staples is NOT a great place to buy cheap padded mailers. For that, go here:

http://www.uline.com

#4 - BURRELLE'S CLIPPING SERVICE

Burrelle's is used by all major PR firms. Their job is to monitor every newspaper and magazine in the country (as well as radio, website and TV transcriptions), and when your name or your band's name shows up, they clip the article and mail the physical copy to your PR firm.

It's a wonderful service to have, and back in the day, before you could find a lot of content online, it was the only real way to monitor the success your publicist was having, but it is VERY expensive. Your publicist pays a high monthly retainer for it (approx. $500) plus about $2 per page per clip.

This means if you are mentioned on the cover of the entertainment section of the newspaper, then there is a photo and lead-in page and then an article on a third page, this can cost you $8. In addition, that article could be syndicated to many outlets and you will pay for copies of the same article (sometimes up to 20 or more).

With the Internet, it is not always necessary to have Burrelle's. But any top notch PR firm will have it and they will charge you for it.

$ Money Saving Tip #4: OK, this one won't get you the same amount of articles that Burrelle's will track because they RULE, but you can opt out of Burrelle's at your PR firm and sign up for Google Alerts:

http://www.google.com/alerts

and have Google track the articles that get placed. You won't get the physical copies of each placement, but if you see an article you really love and need to have, you can always call the subscription department of each newspaper and order a copy for a few bucks.

#5 – GIG EXPENSES –TRANSPORTATION & BEVERAGES

If your publicist and PR team come out to see you play a gig, they could easily bill you for their travel expenses such as cab or subway fare, or gas mileage. And if she brings a music writer to check you out, you could very well be buying that writer drinks at the bar.

So there you have it – the top 5 most frequent visitors on all of my clients' invoices.

$ Money Saving Tip #5: Set A Pre-Negotiated Expenses Budget. You can say: I only want to spend $400 or $500 (or whatever number is comfortable for you) per month on expenses and ask your publicist to suggest ways to keep the number at this budget. So that way you will be completely prepared.

20 CRITICAL WEB 2.0 SITES FOR MUSICIANS

15 Second Pitch

15secondpitch.com helps you define your 15-second elevator pitch and helps you get found in Google searches.

Artist Data

Artistdata.com helps artists publish online information to a variety of destinations from one single portal. You can populate your social networks, official websites, and much more.

Bebo

Bebo.com is the largest social networking site in the UK, Ireland, and New Zealand and it is growing quickly in the United States, Australia and Canada. Bebo has more than 25 million registered members viewing 3.5 billion monthly page views.

Del.icio.us

del.icio.us is a social bookmarking website that is a collection of favorites – yours and everyone else's. You can use del.icio.us to keep links to your favorite articles, blogs, music, reviews, recipes, and more, and access them from any computer. You can use tags to organize and remember your bookmarks.

Digg

Digg.com is all about user-powered content. Everything is submitted and voted on by the Digg community. Share, discover, bookmark, and promote stuff that's important to you.

Eventful

Eventful.com is the world's largest collection of events, taking place in local markets throughout the world, from concerts and sports to singles events and political rallies. They have a great "Demand It" widget as well.

Flickr

Flickr.com is the best online photo management and sharing application in the world. Their goals are to help people make their photos available to the people who matter to them, and to enable new ways of organizing photos. You should maintain a page at Flickr and link it to your Facebook account for extra photo visibility http://www.tinyurl.com/Flickr2Facebook

Hi5

Hi5.com is an online social networking community where bands and fans can create profiles, upload photos and mp3's, and add friends. You can also send and receive messages, upload videos, and form and/or join groups.

Hype Machine

hypem.com is an MP3 & music blog aggregator that scans over 4500 blogs each day, showing you the best songs and blog posts of music on the web – search and discover something new, and if you want to be blogged about, start following featured blogs.

iLike

iLike.com invites every music lover to participate in a more democratic music industry. By rating, recommending, or simply listening to music, you'll impact what gets recommended to others. And they have a great app for Facebook.

imeem

imeem.com is an online community where artists, fans & friends can promote everything: Photos, Albums, Videos, Music, Blogs, Groups, People, and Playlists.

JamBase

JamBase.com is a web portal for all things related to seeing live music, featuring reviews and touring schedules for thousands of artists. Login and create a profile, add your tour dates and get updates on artists you love.

Last.fm

Last.fm lets you to view and edit tags and send recommendations to your friends. Create your own Last.fm stations and tune into personalized radio. Scrobbling a song means that when you listen to it, the name of the song is sent to Last.fm and added to your music profile. Once you've signed up and downloaded Last.fm, you can scrobble songs you listen to on your computer or iPod automatically. Songs you listen to will also appear on your Last.fm profile page for others to see. This helps Last.fm to organize and recommend music to people based on their musical tastes and interests.

MP3 Unsigned

MP3Unsigned.com emphasizes the artists' input into the entire development of the site/community. They are looking for new talent, and have some ambitious plans to promote some of the artists on the site via radio, promotion to record labels, etc.

Ning

Ning.com is an Internet service that allows you to create a social network for anything. You can also join one of the hundreds of thousands of networks built on the platform.

Music Alley from Mevio

music.mevio.com is a pod-safe music network where registered podcast producers can download music to include on their shows. Create a profile and watch Podcasters download and add your tracks to their shows.

Music Think Tank

MusicThinkTank.com is a group blog that brings together key thinkers in the realm of online music business. I am a regular contributor and so is Derek Sivers.

Reverb Nation

ReverbNation.com is designed for artists. Deep, empowering stats and information on your fan base help you make decisions on where to tour and how effectively you are growing your business. Keep your page up to date and export pieces of it to other sites; imagine only having to enter shows one time for all your web locations! And GREAT WIDGETS GALORE!

Twitpic

Twitpic.com allows you to use your mobile phone to snap pictures and they will immediately upload to your Twitter stream (and your Facebook page if you have them connected).

Upcoming

Upcoming.com is a wonderful directory of all events that are going on nationwide, with connections to Yahoo groups and Flickr sites. Upcoming is owned by Yahoo!

THE "NEW" MUSIC BUSINESS DICTIONARY*

Useful definitions you need to know

ARIEL'S FAVORITES *NOT IN ALPHABETICAL ORDER

Blog:

A Blog is really just an informal website. Blog sites are online journals or diaries that are usually more personal and more subjective than a proper website.

Audio-Blog:

An Audio-Blog is a Blog that includes music as well as text. Usually the text is a critique or commentary of the music. Audio-Blogs are becoming more and more embraced by the industry. The Globe & Mail recently ran an in-depth article on Audio-Blogs that makes a great point: "People who maintain music blogs for little glory and no pay want to share their feelings about music, and use MP3 files to make the exchange more vivid."

Blogosphere:

The collective countless blogs on the web (think atmosphere). There are currently over 80 million blogs online.

Podcast:

A podcast, at its core, is an audio file that is created along with some code that enables the file to be downloaded to your computer, where it can be streamed in a player or downloaded to a portable player. There are now thousands of free podcasts available online and at iTunes.

Internet Radio Station:

Listening to radio broadcasts via the Internet using streaming techniques. The audio is played via a software media player or a browser plug-in that supports streaming audio formats such as those from RealNetworks and Microsoft. Internet radio may be streamed at the same time as live AM and FM broadcasts over the air, or it may be a recording of a previous broadcast. In the latter case, selecting the station again after it started will reset the stream to the beginning.

Podsafe:

Podsafe is a term created in the podcasting community to refer to any work which, through its licensing, specifically allows the use of the work in podcasting, regardless of restrictions the same work might have in other realms (Wikipedia).

RSS:

RSS stands for Really Simple Syndication and is a Web feed format used to publish frequently updated content such as blog entries, news headlines or podcasts. RSS solves a problem for people who regularly use the web. It allows you to stay informed easily by retrieving the latest content from the sites you are interested in. You save time by not needing to visit each site individually. You ensure your privacy by not needing to join each site's email newsletter. The number of sites offering RSS feeds is growing rapidly and includes big names.

Wiki:

(from oreilly.net) A wiki is a website where users can add, remove, and edit every page using a web browser. It's so terrifically easy for people to jump in and revise pages that wikis are becoming known as the tool of choice for large, multiple-participant projects.

RSS Reader / Feed Reader:

RSS content can be read using software called a "feed reader" or an "aggregator" such as Google Reader. The user subscribes to a feed by entering the feed's link into the reader or by clicking an RSS icon in a browser that initiates the subscription process. The Icon looks like this:

 Click on it to subscribe to anything you want.

Tagging:

A tag is a (relevant) keyword or term associated with or assigned to a piece of information (e.g. a picture, article, or video clip), thus describing the item. Tags are usually chosen informally and personally by the author/creator or the consumer of the item. Tags are typically used for resources such as computer files, web pages, digital images, and Internet bookmarks (both in social bookmarking services, and in the current generation of web browsers). For this reason, "tagging" has become associated with the Web 2.0 buzz (wikipedia).

Keyword:

A keyword is the term used for words included in a web page that would match words used by web surfers in finding that web page (via a search engine). Keywords can simply be words included in the body text of the document, or added to the header using meta tags to increase the number of keywords (your web designer can easily do this). Selecting keywords, that match your target audience's use of the web is a critical marketing tactic. (definethat.com)

ABOUT ARIEL HYATT

Ariel Hyatt is the founder of *Ariel Publicity & Cyber PR,* a New York-based digital firm that connects artists, authors and filmmakers to blogs, podcasts, Internet radio stations and social media sites. Over the past 13 years her firm has represented over 1,400 musicians from all musical genres. In 2009 the company expanded to handle campaigns for authors and filmmakers as well.

Educating musicians is Ariel's passion and her philosophy is: combine social media with Internet marketing to help artists grow their fan bases and increase their income.

Several times a year, Ariel leads sold-out workshops for musicians and music industry professionals looking to learn about social media and online marketing. Her bi-weekly E-zine and YouTube series *Sound Advice* has over 10,000 subscribers and the list is steadily growing.

Ariel has written dozens of articles on how to navigate the new music business and her book, *Music Success in Nine Weeks,* is in its second edition.

She is a contributing blogger to Music Think Tank and has spoken at countless music conferences over the years including: SXSW, CMJ, The Future of Music, ECMAs & OCFF (Canada), NARAS, The Taxi Road Rally and The BMI Music Panel Series.

Ariel also proudly serves on the boards of SoundCtrl, a music and technology event platform for the convergence of music and digital media, and the Sweet Relief Musicians Fund.

CYBER PR WEBSITES

Ariel Publicity & Cyber PR

http://www.ArielPublicity.com

Music Success in Nine Weeks

http://www.MusicSuccessInNineWeeks.com

Cyber PR For Musicians

http://www.CyberPRMusic.com

Ariel's 2x Per Month Sound Advice Newsletter delivered to you

http://www.soundadviceezine.com

Watch Sound Advice TV

http://www.YouTube.com/ArielPublicity

Cyber PR For Authors

http://www.CyberPRBooks.com

Cyber PR For Filmmakers

http://www.SideLotStudio.com

PRODUCTS AVAILABLE FROM CYBER PR

Music Success in Nine Weeks – Book (or eBook)

A step-by-step guide that walks you through how to supercharge your publicity, build your fan base, and earn more money. This book breaks down exactly how to achieve these goals in a week-by-week syllabus with written exercises.

> "You need to buy this book, now! It's the only one that directly answers: 'I've got great music, but now what?' Read it, and you'll be earning its value back ten-fold."

~ Derek Sivers, Founder, CD Baby

Each book comes with: A lifetime membership to Ariel's exclusive online closed Mastermind Forum where you can join the community of artists working with the book and being coached by Ariel and her team.

» http://www.MusicSuccessInNineWeeks.com

Review You

A guaranteed CD review, written by a professional music blogger, delivered to you within 14 days. *Review You* covers all genres of music.

> "I tried for months to get my CD reviewed. I read everything I could find on the subject and used their suggestions to the letter. After 20 mailings I received one review back – about three months later! There are so many of us out there that it's become increasingly harder to get our material reviewed. Thank God for ReviewYou.com!! The review I received from their staff writer was fantastic and gave me a lot to think about – and it was done in two weeks! This is a service that I will use over & over again."

~ Paul Rader/Independent Solo Artist

» Order your review now at: http://www.reviewyou.com

Musician's Web & Social Media Audio 2.0 Bootcamp

This four-hour, 5-CD audio course will teach you how to use the newest social media tools available online and how to combine them with traditional marketing techniques to increase your overall footprint online, attract fans and transform your website from web 1.0 to web 2.0. It also includes an overview of all elements of Web 2.0/Social Media and its uses for musicians, including: podcasting, social networking, and blogging.

This course comes with a workbook that highlights the most memorable points and is crammed with useful links and resources, including Ariel's list of 20 Web 2.0 sites to help you increase your online presence. Special bonus: *Magic Words That Sell More Music* – a 16-page booklet that will walk you through the basics of copy writing, headline writing and how to make people want to buy from your website.

» http://www.arielpublicity.com/web2bootcamp

CYBER PR CAMPAIGNS

Cyber PR Gets Your Music Featured on Blogs, Podcasts, Internet Radio Stations, and More.

Ariel's firm represents musicians of all genres and from all over the world. Click here: http://www.cyberprmusic.com or call the office to find out how we can get your music into the hands of thousands of online social media makers.

(212) 239-8384

"Hiring Ariel Publicity was by far and in large the best money my band ever spent. Ariel starts right away and within days we had more publicity than our record label's publicity company had gotten us since we signed... worth every penny."

~ Jeffrey Todd, Fort Pastor

"Ariel has incomparable reach. Less than one month into my campaign, I've already been played around the world, in Australia, England, the US, the Netherlands, and more. I've already come across in-depth reviews of my debut album from widely-distributed bloggers to which I would otherwise have no contact. No effort is wasted, and I can follow the campaign, in detail, in real time. It's incredible, and it's working."

~ Trey Green

MUSICIAN'S PUBLICITY BOOTCAMP

Co-hosted with Bob Baker of *The Buzz Factor,* this four-hour, 5-CD audio course will teach you the nuts and bolts of traditional publicity, and it's filled with insider secrets on how to reach the music media and get the exposure you deserve!

Learn Ariel's rules for following up with the media (it took her years to get this right), clever ways to get past media gatekeepers (receptionists, voice mail, etc.), and the top 3 mistakes most musicians make when preparing their press kits — and how to avoid them.

You also get a 70-minute bonus audio collection featuring in-depth music PR Q&A sessions with attendees, a 35-page Bonus Workbook filled with publicity checklists, articles, and music PR resource lists – plus a 26-page killer collection of media kit and press release samples, including bios, tour date announcements, fact sheets, cover letters, one sheets, and more.

» http://www.arielpublicity.com/prbootcamp

MORE USEFUL WEB DEFINITIONS (THIS TIME IN ALPHABETICAL ORDER) FROM A GREAT SITE : WWW.TVB.ORG

Avatar:

Graphic representation of a person online, usually used to navigate a virtual world such as Second Life. Some try to make their avatars look like themselves, and others go for idealized/stylized visions.

Folksonomy:

A group of people cooperating spontaneously to organize information into categories.

HTML:

Stands for "Hyper Text Markup Language". The language used to develop and create webpages.

Hyperlink:

A graphic or word that when clicked will open another document. Hyperlinks are the primary way to navigate between webpages and websites.

Mashup:

A web service or software tool that combines two or more tools to create a whole new service. The term is also used to describe user generated remixes of content from different sources.

Newsgroup:

A virtual area on the Internet reserved for the discussion of a particular topic.

Newsreader:

Gathers the news from multiple blogs or news sites via RSS, allowing readers to access news from a single web site or program. Online newsreaders (like Bloglines, Pluck, or Newsgator) are web sites that allow you to read RSS feeds from within your web browser.

Opt In:

A direct, proactive request by an individual email recipient to have their email address added to a specific mailing list.

Opt Out:

An email subscription practice by which users request to be deleted from an email distribution list by either selecting a link, or sending an email that requests their address be deleted.

Server:

A computer that houses websites and is connected to the Internet 24 hours a day.

Social Bookmarking:

The ability to save and categorize a personal collection of bookmarks and share them with others. Users may also take bookmarks saved by others and add them to their own collection, as well as to subscribe to the lists of others.

Social Media:

Online technologies and practices that people use to share opinions, insights, experiences, and perspectives with each other.

Social Networking:

Websites that allow people to link to others to share opinions, insights experiences and perspectives, whether it's music fans on MySpace, business contacts on LinkedIn, or classmates on Facebook. Many media sites have adopted social networking features such as blogs, message boards, podcasts and wikis to help build online communities around their content.

Streaming Media:

Video or audio transmitted over a network that users can begin to play immediately instead of waiting for the entire file to download. RealMedia, QuickTime and Windows Media are the most common streaming formats.

Tags:

Keywords attached to photos or web pages to help identify them and allow them to show up in search engines.

URL:

Stands for "Uniform Resource Locator". A string that supplies the Internet address of a website or page on the World Wide Web.

Viral Marketing:

Any marketing technique that induces websites or users to pass on a marketing message to other sites or users.

Viral Video:

Video content, usually humorous in nature, made popular through sharing, typically through email or media sharing websites.

Vlog:

Video-based journals posted online.

Web 2.0:

The transition of the World Wide Web from a collection of websites to a full-fledged computing platform serving web applications to end users.

Web 3.0:

The evolution of Web usage and interaction along several separate paths, including transforming the Web into a database, and a move towards making content accessible by multiple non-browser applications.

Webcasting:

Communicating to multiple computers at the same time over internet by "streaming" live audio and/or live video through compression and decompression of the signal.

Webisode:

A short video available only on the Web.

Widget:

A third party item that can be embedded in a web page.

Wiki:

A website or similar online resource which allows users to add and edit content collectively.

NOTES

NOTES

NOTES

NOTES